PICKING THE "RIGHT" BIBLE STUDY PROGRAM

By Sr. Macrina Scott, O.S.F.

ACTA Publications

Chicago, Illinois

PICKING THE "RIGHT" BIBLE STUDY PROGRAM
Reviews of 92 Recommended Programs
With a listing of the top 15

by Sr. Macrina Scott, O.S.F.

This book is dedicated to Robert B. Scott, my father and the strongest supporter of my work in making God's word alive and active in the church today. Rooted deeply in the pre-Vatican II Catholic Church, he welcomed with enthusiasm every new work of the Spirit.

Editing by Rita Benz, B.V.M. and Gregory F. Augustine Pierce
Cover design by John Dylong
Typesetting by Jean Lachowicz

Copyright © 1992 by **ACTA Publications**
4848 N. Clark Street
Chicago, IL 60640
312-271-1030

ISBN: 0-87946-063-6

Printed in the United States of America

Contents

Foreword

It does not seem so long ago, maybe 15 years. I was leading a workshop on the New Testament for a large gathering of Catholics--priests, religious, laypeople--in the heart of Missouri. During the noon break, I went to a barbershop and waited my turn for a haircut. It was an old-fashioned barbershop with a barber pole outside, a place everybody went to sit and talk.

As I walked in, everyone fell silent, and I felt very much a stranger, which I was. After a while, the barber looked up at me and asked, "Stranger in town?" I told him I was and ventured what had brought me there. Somebody nodded. Somebody else blurted out, "The Catholics are studying the Bible?" Comments and murmurs from everybody.

For Catholics to be studying the Bible was not the ordinary thing. For the Baptist population in that area it was something to wonder about.

Now Catholic Bible study is far more ordinary, and this book by Sister Macrina Scott testifies to that. Sister Macrina is the founder and director of the Catholic Biblical School in the Archdiocese of Denver. In her position, she has had plenty of opportunity to use and test the growing number of resources for Bible study groups.

The book distills Sister Macrina's experience, both direct and indirect, with those resources and presents her judgement as to their suitability and helpfulness for various groups and contexts. As she shows, some resources are fine for the more advanced, while others are best for beginners. Besides, not all have the same purpose. Some are more pastorally suited than others.

While a large and growing number of Catholics is very much interested in Bible study, many do not know where to turn for help in their study. Sister Macrina's reviews of many resource programs for Bible study can help everyone who asks, "What is really good? What do scholars and experienced teachers of the Bible recommend?"

As Catholics continue to study the Bible and become more biblically literate, the phenomenon of Catholics studying the Bible will eventually be taken for granted, even in a Bible Belt barbershop.

The Bible belongs to all of us, and all must come to understand it, enjoy it, and benefit from it.

Eugene LaVerdiere, S.S.S.
Senior Editor, *Emmanuel* Magazine

A Note on Background and Criteria

For the past nine years, I have had the privilege of being the director of the Catholic Biblical School of the Archdiocese of Denver, an intensive, four year program aimed at training lay people so thoroughly in scripture that they are qualified to lead Bible study groups in their own parishes or small Christian communities.

When our graduates begin to offer biblical study opportunities for their fellow parishioners who may not be ready to commit themselves to a program as intensive as ours, they often come to me for help in selecting the Bible study program they should use. It has been a major frustration for me not to be able to advise them as well or as specifically as I should. As anyone involved in Bible study knows well, there are now hundreds of programs of extremely varied quality on the market There is no way to evaluate a given program without reading or viewing it completely. Few ministers or lay leaders have the expertise in current biblical scholarship and adult education methodology to judge the relative worth of the many programs available. Fewer still have the time to study thoroughly even a handful of them.

Consequently, selection of bible study material is often made in a random and serendipitous manner--based on what might be available in a local book store, what might appear in a publisher's catalog or advertisement, or what might be mentioned by a friend or colleague. It seemed to me that this problem was more than a local Denver issue and that it was not just a "Catholic" problem.

I therefore applied for and received a grant from the Chicago-based Foundation for Adult Catechetical Teaching Aids which funded a nine-month sabbatical that allowed me time to review a great many currently available Bible study programs. I have done my best with the time and material available to me. Omissions and errors undoubtedly appear, and I hope that readers and publishers will point them out to me. (A form is provided in the back of the book for this purpose.)

I pray that with the Spirit guiding me I have written something that will be useful to all those searching for the "right" Bible study program. God's blessing on your search.

Macrina Scott, O.S.F.
Catholic Biblical School
Denver, Colorado

How This Book is Helpful in Selecting a Bible Study Program

If you are beginning a Bible study group, or beginning a new topic in an ongoing group, it is very important for you to select a program that fits the needs of your particular group. A program that is too challenging will discourage members; one that is not sufficiently challenging will bore them. A program which requires preparation for each session will not work properly if many in your group are unwilling to prepare. And so on.

How can you find what is right for you without spending thousands of hours going through the hundreds of available programs? Most available information comes from publishers, and it is in the nature of things that each publishing house wants its products used by everybody, so they are not overly helpful in the selection process. This book attempts to provide as much information as possible to assist you. It also includes evaluative comments which, while they make no claim to infallibility, at least come from an educator with wide experience in adult biblical education and no axe to grind.

Here is the way in which your questions are answered in this book: some in the heading (information immediately following the program title, before the review proper), the review (the paragraphs following the heading), the questions (standard questions which follow each review), or in one of the special listings found in the Table of Contents.

How do I find the review of a program or series in which my group is interested? If you know the title of the program or series, consult the Index that begins on p. 239. Otherwise, look on p. 13 for studies including both Testaments, p. 63 for studies on the Old Testament, and p. 103 for those on the New Testament.

Is this a good program? Look in the review for evaluation, and look on p.5 for the "Fifteen Favorites" which seemed to this reviewer to be of particularly outstanding quality.

Is the theology in this program acceptable? Many of the Bible study materials on the market have a strong fundamentalist bias. None of these are included in this book. The reviewer, reading from a Roman Catholic point of view, indicates in the reviews any specific teaching in the book which seemed contrary to Catholic teaching, and any pronounced emphasis on Catholic issues which might make the program unsuitable for Protestants. Where the program has official Roman Catholic approval, this is indicated by "imprimatur" in the heading.

Will this program suit my particular group? Note particularly the last question, "Participants required to prepare for each session?" It is very important to be clear about whether or not your group is committed to preparation, and to use a corresponding program. Note that some programs do not require preparation for the session, but recommend homework as a follow-up to each session. In these cases, individuals who do not do the homework can benefit from the session and will not hold the group back, even though they will not themselves experience the full benefit of the program.

There are special lists of programs suited to these types of groups: Beginning, Advanced, Peace and Justice (p.7); Women's Issues, Prayer, Men, Lunch hour or other groups meeting less than one hour (p.8); Nursing Homes, Spanish Language (p.9).

More information will be found in the review.

Who wrote the program? The heading lists authors, unless more than two for a particular program are named. If you are looking for a particular author, check in the index at the back of the book.

How much does it cost? This information is given in the heading, but should be checked with the publisher due to ever changing prices.

How can I get it? Try your local bookstore, but you may have to write the publisher, who is listed in the heading. Publishers' addresses are given on p.237.

When was it published? A significant question, since no book can include developments of biblical scholarship later than its date of publication. Look in the heading.

How long is the program? The number of sessions recommended is stated in the heading to give you a general idea, though some programs can be adapted to various lengths.

Will I need audio or video tapes? Look in the heading, or look for lists of programs using tapes on p.11.

Is this program part of a series? This is a very important question in using this book. If a program is part of a series, at the end of the review there is a note saying "**See:___**" This refers you to a description of the series. Be sure to read this. All information which applies to the whole series is to be found only there; the individual review includes only the details in which this program differs from others in the series.

How can I find a program about the particular biblical book in which my group is interested? Look on p. 63 for a list of Old Testament books and on p. 103 for those in the New Testament. Also, see Little Rock Scripture Study Program, p.217, and Scripture Share and Prayer, p.225, which have more programs on specific biblical books than it has been possible to review in this book.

What reference books do I need besides the program itself? Some possibilities are listed on p.231. If you already have reference books not listed there, ask someone knowledgeable about scripture if they are reliable.

What kind of preparation does the leader need? In all programs, the leader needs some skill in facilitation. Questions 9 and 10 tell you whether or not practical directions and biblical background are provided for leaders. Read the review for further comments. If you want some assistance as a leader, see the leadership training material listed on p.233.

Does this program incorporate up to date historical-critical scholarship? See question 1. Programs in total contradiction to such scholarship are not included in this book, but some programs, especially those oriented to prayer, take an approach which neither contradicts scholarship nor utilizes it.

Is there an emphasis on background information? See question 2.

Is there an emphasis on application to personal and family life? See question 3.

Is there application to the life and mission of the church? See question 4.

Is there application to broader social issues? See question 5.

Is sexist language used? This may be an important question if you wish a variety of people to be comfortable in your group. Question 6 tells whether generic masculines are used by the author of the program. If sexist language is avoided to the point of never referring to God as masculine, or of changing language in quotations, this is generally noted in the review.

Does the program give guidance for prayer during meetings? See question 7.

Are discussion questions included? See question 8.

Does this program presume that group members already know something about scripture? See question 12, and list of programs particularly suited to beginning and advanced groups, p. 7.

What does it look like? All printed materials are paperback. See heading for number and size of pages.

Each review is presented on one or two pages. All pages are perforated for easy removal, and permission is granted to reproduce individual reviews for internal group consideration in picking the "right" Bible study program.

Fifteen Favorites   (in alphabetical order)

Of the hundreds of programs reviewed for this book, these fifteen seemed to the reviewer to stand out for their excellence. No program, of course, is suitable for every group. See the individual reviews to find out the kinds of groups for which these are recommended. (If a title is part of a series, this is indicated in parentheses.)

1. The Apostle Paul: Male Chauvinist or Proponent of Equality? p.171

2. Blessed by the God of Abraham, Isaac, and Jacob
   (Bless Bible Studies) p.65

3. Breaking Open the Gospel of Luke p.155

4. Come Follow Me p.37

5. Come Holy Spirit p.43

6. Food for the Journey p.23

7. Getting to Know the Bible. p.25

8. God of Our Mothers p.59

9. Isaiah (Friendship Bible Study) p.93

10. Jesus and the Gospels (Paulist Bible Study Program) p.127

11. Peacemaking (Small-Group Bible Study) p.55

12. The Pilgrim God: A Biblical Journey p.73

13. Psalms (Covenant Bible Study) p.99

14. Questions of Christians: Vol. 2, Matthew's Response
    (Questions of Christians) p.147

15. Writings of St.Paul (De Sales Program) p.189

These programs are marked with an asterisk (*) throughout this book.

Programs Recommended for Specific Groups

Different Bible study programs are appropriate for different groups. These lists take into consideration various group interests and levels of expertise in studying the scriptures. (If a title is part of a series, this is indicated in parentheses.)

Recommended for Beginners
Acts of the Apostles (Little Rock), p.167
Basic Tools for Bible Study (De Sales), p.15
Beginners' Guide to Bible Sharing, Vol. 1, p.105
The Bible: A Simple Introduction, p.17
The Book of Jonah: A Study Guide, p.91
Flight to Freedom (Small-Group Bible Study), p.77
*Food for the Journey, p.23
*Getting to Know the Bible, p.25
A Guide to Reading the Old Testament,Part One p.67
Hand Me Another Brick: Nehemiah (Charles Swindoll) p.85
How to Read and Pray the Gospels, p.123
Jonah and Ruth (Friendship Bible Study), p.71
Joseph: From Pit to Pinnacle (Charles Swindoll), p.83
Walking Together through the Bible, p.33

Recommended for Advanced Groups
Acts - Paul's Early and Great Letters (Scripture Share and Prayer), p.169
The Bible Makes Sense, p.35
Biblical Woman, p.57
Harper's New American Bible Study Program, p.45
Interpreting Scripture, p.47
*The Pilgrim God, p.73
Pre-Exilic Prophets (Scripture Share and Prayer), p.95
Rolling Back the Rock, p.141
The Way of the Lord, p.117

Groups Concerned with Peace and Justice Issues
Adults Approach "the Revelation", p.197
Amos and Hosea (Men's Bible Studies) p.89
*Come Follow Me, p.37
*Come Holy Spirit , p.43
Love and Justice: A Biblical Understanding (Covenant Bible Studies), p.51
*Peacemaking (Small-Group Bible Studies), p.53
*Psalms (Covenant Bible Studies), p.99
Revelation (Men's Bible Studies), p.201
Unexpected News, p.41
Walking Together through the Bible, p.33

Groups Concerned with Women's Issues
*The Apostle Paul: Male Chauvinist or Proponent of Equality? p.171
Biblical Woman, p.57
*God of Our Mothers: Seven Biblical Women Tell Their Stories, p.59
Women, Men, and the Bible, p.61

Groups Concerned with Biblical Prayer
*Food for the Journey, p.23
*God of Our Mothers: Seven Biblical Women Tell Their Stories, p.59
How to Read and Pray the Gospels, p.123
Involving Adults in the Bible, p.125
Visualizing Scripture, p.143

Men's Groups
Amos and Hosea (Men's Bible Studies), p.89
1 and 2 Corinthians (Men's Bible Studies), p.175
Hebrews (Men's Bible Studies), p.179
Psalms (Men's Bible Studies), p.101
Revelation (Men's Bible Studies), p.201

Lunch Hour Groups
These are programs planned for sessions of under one hour, and may be appropriate for any group meeting for a short period.
Amos and Hosea (Men's Bible Studies), p.89
*The Apostle Paul: Male Chauvinist or Proponent of Equality? p.171
Benziger New Testament Study Series. p.205
*Come Follow Me, p.37
1 and 2 Corinthians (Men's Bible Studies), p.175
Discovering the Gospels, p.121
*God of Our Mothers: Seven Biblical Women Tell Their Stories, p.59
Hebrews (Men's Bible Studies), p.179
*Isaiah (Friendship Bible Studies), p.93
1, 2, and 3 John (Friendship Bible Studies), p.191
Jonah and Ruth (Friendship Bible Studies), p.71
The Life of David (Covenant Bible Studies), p.87
Love and Justice: A Biblical Understanding (Covenant Bible Studies), p.51
Parables (Friendship Bible Studies), p.139
Proverbs (Friendship Bible Studies), p.97
*Psalms (Covenant Bible Studies), p.99
Psalms (Men's Bible Studies), p.101
Revelation (Men's Bible Studies), p.201
Seasons of Faith, p.39
Sermon on the Mount (Covenant Bible Studies), p.149

Programs Utilizing Audio or Video Tapes

Audio Tapes

Acts--Paul's Early and Great Letters (Scripture Share and Prayer), p.169
God of Our Mothers: Seven Biblical Women Tell Their Stories, p.59
Pre-Exilic Prophets (Scripture Share and Prayer), p.95
Questions of Christians: Vol.1. Mark's Response, p.153
Questions of Christians: Vol.2 Matthew's Response, p.147
Questions of Christians: Vol.3 Luke's Response, p.159
Questions of Christians: Vol.4, John's Response, p.163
Scripture Foundations (Scripture Share and Prayer), p.31

Video Tapes

Basic Tools for Bible Study (De Sales), p.15
Come, Follow Me, p.37
Israel Becomes a People (Paulist), p.79
Jesus and the Gospels (Paulist), p.127
The Living Gospels (De Sales), p.133
Rolling Back the Rock, p.141
The Story of the Old Testament Covenant (De Sales), p.75
The Writings of St.Paul (De Sales), p.189

Reviews of Individual Programs

ASIC TOOLS FOR BIBLE STUDY.

e Sales Program. Franciscan Communications, 1987. imprimatur. 4 videos, each
ntaining 2 sessions, 1 hour each session. $385 for videos, facilitator's guide, and 1
rticipant's manual. $6.50 for each additional participant's manual, 139 pp., 8 ½ 11.
sessions.

e title may be misleading. This program aims at introducing Catholics with no
owledge of the Bible to the basic methods of modern biblical scholarship. It is a
ntle introduction, taking care to shock as little as possible and to integrate new
formation into traditional Catholic experience. It emphasizes that biblical study is
w to Catholics and deals with the problems it can raise, trying at the same time to
ow that it can be spiritually enriching.

pics covered include inspiration, the development of the canon, translations,
blical geography and archeology, biblical history, biblical criticism and interpre-
tion, the Book of Revelation, and biblical spirituality. The lectures might be used
parately, especially the one on geography and that on Revelation.

vast assortment of information is included here. It is suitable for an audience
ngry for information, troubled by modern biblical scholarship, and not yet ready
study the biblical text itself. Participants are encouraged toward reading the Bible
d praying from it, but not forced.

he discussion questions may not elicit much discussion.

hile the information given is generally good, a few points seem misleading. We
e told that there are six deuterocanonical books instead of seven. The discussion
translations seems quite inadequate, recommending only the New American
ble, and treating the Living Bible as if it were a translation rather than a paraphrase.
hen the text from Isaiah about the "virgin shall conceive" is discussed, participants
e never told that the word "virgin" does not appear in the Hebrew. Moses is said
have led the Israelites out of Egypt exactly at the time of Akhenaton, a dating with
hich few mainline scholars would agree.

timeline and other useful charts are included, but no maps.

ee: **De Sales Program, p.211.**

1. Up-to-date historical critical scholarship incorporated? **Yes**

2. Background information emphasized? **Yes**

3. Application to personal and family life emphasized? **No**

4. Application to the life and mission of the church included? **Yes**

5. Application to broader social issues included? **Yes**

6. Sexist language avoided? **Yes**

7. Guidance for prayer at group meetings provided? **Yes**

8. Discussion questions provided? **Yes**

9. Practical directions for group leaders provided? **Yes**

10. Biblical background for group leaders provided? **No**

11. Biblical background for group members presumed? **No**

12. Participants required to prepare for each session? **No**

HE BIBLE: A SIMPLE INTRODUCTION.
mes Auer and Robert Delaney. Franciscan Communications, 1988. imprimatur. 15
)., 8 ½ x 11. $1.25. A Study Guide to a Minicourse in Reading the Bible, a Simple
troduction. 10 pp., 5 ½ x 8 ½. $ .35.

iis is a well written and colorfully illustrated article for beginners, high school
udents or adults who want a quick introduction to the Bible. It touches on
thorship, revelation, inspiration, inerrancy, literary style, symbolism, tradition,
e canon, the Old Testament, and the New Testament. It also contains a chronologi-
l chart showing when the biblical books were written, and some advice for persons
•ginning to read the Bible. Not everyone will agree that Matthew is the best starting
ace for those with no previous knowledge of scripture. It might be argued that
•me are likely to be bored by the long discourses and to get a false understanding
the Old Testament by learning of it first from Matthew.

ie Minicourse booklet seems to be designed for a teacher who wants to base a class
· classes on the article. Nine discussion questions are scattered through the booklet.
ot all groups will be stirred to much discussion by questions such as "How do you
ink Christians can make God's Word come alive in today's society?" or "What
roblem in reading Scripture is common among Christian churches today that do not
cognize the indwelling activity of the Spirit in the church which Catholics refer to
i `Tradition'?" It suggests appropriate scripture readings as background for the
ticle, and gives additional suggestions for reading the scripture and a list of
nportant biblical passages.

is not clear exactly how these materials are intended to be used, but a creative
acher could probably find a way to utilize them either with an RCIA or other group
tat wants to spend only three or four hours getting an introduction to scripture, or
ith a group that wants to spend a little time on an introduction before digging into
specific biblical book.

1.	Up-to-date historical critical scholarship incorporated?	**Yes**
2.	Background information emphasized?	**Yes**
3.	Application to personal and family life emphasized?	**No**
4.	Application to the life and mission of the church included?	**Yes**
5.	Application to broader social issues included?	**Yes**
6.	Sexist language avoided?	**Yes**

7. Guidance for prayer at group meetings provided?   No

8. Discussion questions provided?   Yes

9. Practical directions for group leaders provided?   No

10. Biblical background for group leaders provided?   No

11. Biblical background for group members presumed?   No

12. Participants required to prepare for each session?   Yes

ISCOVERING THE BIBLE: 8 SIMPLE KEYS
OR LEARNING AND PRAYING.
OOK ONE.

hn Tickle. Liguori, 1978. imprimatur. 112 pp., 8 ½ x 11. $3.95. Leader's Guide by arilyn Norquist, 64 pp., 5 x 7 ¼. $2.95. 17 sessions.

iis is a very simple overview of scripture aimed at high school students or very isophisticated adults. Each chapter of the participant's book includes a drawing eant to summarize the main ideas, a page or two of input, a list of related scripture ferences to be looked up and discussed, a brief prayer service (scripture reading, iuse, responsorial psalm, prayer), and "discussion questions" which actually ask irticipants to remember what was said in the input.

ie themes covered are: revelation, election, covenant, law, sin, redemption, essiah, and love. One session is given to the Old Testament and one to the New estament teaching on each theme. The tendency is to reduce the rich concreteness scripture to generalities. The color and dynamism get lost in the process of immarizing into general concepts. Little use is made of the enrichment available m contemporary scholarship.

ie Leader's Guide is a valuable addition. It provides suggestions for the Leader's vn prayer (more varied and creative than the prayer services in the participant's ok), many practical suggestions, and, most important, a few real discussion iestions aimed at bringing the personal experience of participants into the study. also provides a little additional input for the leader.

is not altogether clear how the material in the two books is to be combined in each ssion. It would take a creative leader to bring it all to life. The leader should also ive a good biblical background to answer questions and assist in the discussion.

ee also: Discovering the Bible: Simple Keys for Learning and Praying.
Book Two, p.21.

1. Up-to-date historical critical scholarship incorporated?   **Yes**

2. Background information emphasized?   **No**

3. Application to personal and family life emphasized?   **Yes**

4. Application to the life and mission of the church included?   **Yes**

5. Application to broader social issues included?   **No**

6. Sexist language avoided?   **No**

7. Guidance for prayer at group meetings provided?   **Yes**

8. Discussion questions provided?   **Yes**

9. Practical directions for group leaders provided?   **Yes**

10. Biblical background for group leaders provided?   **Yes**

11. Biblical background for group members presumed?   **No**

12. Participants required to prepare for each session?   **No**

Studies Including Both Testaments
Introductions (For Beginners)

DISCOVERING THE BIBLE:
SIMPLE KEYS FOR LEARNING AND PRAYING.
BOOK TWO.

John Tickle. Liguori, 1980. imprimatur. 96 pp., 8 ½ x 11. $3.95. Leader's Guide by Leslie R. Keylock, 80 pp., 5 x 7 ¼. $2.95. 16 sessions.

In the same format as Book One, this volume deals with the themes: community, hospitality, faith, worship, holiness, justice, suffering, discipleship.

The input is considerably more down to earth, and the discussion questions for each session include several applying the theme to participants' lives. This is considerably better adapted to use by Bible study groups than Book One, and it can easily be used without having used Book One.

The Leader's Guide is quite different from that for Book One, and is geared primarily to teachers of high school classes. A few ideas might be gleaned from it for leaders of adult groups.

See: **Discovering the Bible: Simple Keys for Learning and Praying. Book One. p.19.**

1.	Up-to-date historical critical scholarship incorporated?	Yes
2.	Background information emphasized?	No
3.	Application to personal and family life emphasized?	Yes
4.	Application to the life and mission of the church included?	Yes
5.	Application to broader social issues included?	Yes
6.	Sexist language avoided?	No
7.	Guidance for prayer at group meetings provided?	Yes
8.	Discussion questions provided?	Yes
9.	Practical directions for group leaders provided?	No
10.	Biblical background for group leaders provided?	No
11.	Biblical background for group members presumed?	No
12.	Participants required to prepare for each session?	No

FOOD FOR THE JOURNEY:
XPLORING SCRIPTURE FOR CATECHESIS IN THE RCIA.
nes V. Parker. Ave Maria, 1989. 187 pp., 7 x 10. $8.95. 16 sessions.

is program is intended to provide catechumens with a basic knowledge of the
blical story as background to the lectionary readings. It can provide the same
rvice for persons who are not catechumens, but lack basic biblical background. It
o teaches catechumens, and others, to pray over the scripture and to share their
perience of the word in small groups.

rticipants commit to spend half an hour daily at prayerful reflection and journaling
 an assigned chapter of the Bible. The book provides brief introductions and two
estions for reflection each day.

hen the group meets they share their reflections from the previous week. Then the
der gives a fifteen minute presentation to introduce the readings for the coming
ek, and the group discusses one of the stories they will be reading.

e program is oriented to prayer more than study, but ideally the leader should
ve some biblical background and speaking ability. The commentary is based on
ntemporary biblical scholarship, though this is never flaunted.

e readings are carefully selected to introduce the highpoints of the biblical story
d to encourage personal reflection. The brief introductory material ties the stories
gether, provides some minimum essential background information, and makes
nnections between the Old and New Testaments. Wisely, the Old Testament story
old beginning with Abraham, and the myths of Genesis 1-11 are treated at the end.
 that time participants have met other stories which are not historical (Jonah,
ther, Judith) and are less likely to be shocked by the literary form of the creation
count than they would have been had it been dealt with first.

velve sessions deal with the Old Testament and four with the Gospels. The
roductory material about the gospels is particularly good, showing how surpris-
g are the parables, the actions of Jesus, and the resurrection.

rticipants should also be encouraged to read the 20 pages of introduction, which
ve an excellent and very readable orientation to the Catholic approach to scripture.

rticipants will come away with an overview of the biblical story. But the daily
ayer on strategic passages will give life to the content and enable it to be assimilated
 a way that a usual overview is not. Most important, habits of reflection and
aring on scripture will be firmly rooted. This is a valuable program for any parish,

and should not be limited to catechumens.

1. Up-to-date historical critical scholarship incorporated? **Yes**

2. Background information emphasized? **No**

3. Application to personal and family life emphasized? **Yes**

4. Application to the life and mission of the church included? **Yes**

5. Application to broader social issues included? **Yes**

6. Sexist language avoided? **Yes**

7. Guidance for prayer at group meetings provided? **No**

8. Discussion questions provided? **Yes**

9. Practical directions for group leaders provided? **Yes**

10. Biblical background for group leaders provided? **No**

11. Biblical background for group members presumed? **No**

12. Participants required to prepare for each session? **Yes**

Studies Including Both Testaments

Introductions (For Beginners)

* GETTING TO KNOW THE BIBLE.

Melvin L. Farrell, S.S. (Hi-Time, 1984). imprimatur. 112 pp., 5 x 8. $5.95. Discussion Guide, Kathleen A. Mulvey. (Hi-Time, 1984). 64 pp., 5½ x 8½. $3.50. 20 - 24 sessions.

Father Farrell provides an excellent overview of the Bible in 24 chapters, four pages each, easy to read, and enlivened with contemporary examples in text and photographs. Helpful maps and charts add to the visual attractiveness of the booklet. The author takes nothing for granted and explains clearly the difference between Catholic and fundamentalist approaches to the Bible. His use of church documents and his whole approach is reassuring to Catholics unacquainted with biblical scholarship who might be shocked by a less sensitive presentation of the same material.

Kathleen Mulvey has provided an outstanding discussion leader's guide. For each session it contains: brief opening and closing prayers, a summary of the contents of Father Farrell's article, plenty of excellent discussion questions, and an activity. The activities are an unusual and very well developed element in the program. For the first several sessions they are aimed at getting participants familiar with the basic skills of finding their way around their Bibles. Later, very creative activities are described, usually actual studies of the relevant scripture passages.

While some very good suggestions are given on techniques for the leader, there are no additional biblical background or suggestions for reading to obtain it. A leader would need some biblical background and teaching skills to facilitate these activities successfully.

Participants are not expected to read from the Bible itself except during the activities. The program could be greatly strengthened by encouraging participants to read relevant biblical passages after each session. A leader wishing to encourage such reading would have to select the passages.

Since the articles are so short, they could be read either in advance or at the beginning of the session. A group desiring to meet fewer than 24 times could probably cover two chapters during a two-hour session for the first eight chapters, which are introductory material. Chapter nine begins a rapid coverage of the highpoints of the Bible, and it would be difficult to cover more than one chapter at a time.

1. Up-to-date historical critical scholarship incorporated? **Yes**

2. Background information emphasized? **Yes**

3. Application to personal and family life emphasized? **Yes**

4. Application to the life and mission of the church included? **Yes**

5. Application to broader social issues included? **Yes**

6. Sexist language avoided? **Yes**

7. Guidance for prayer at group meetings provided? **Yes**

8. Discussion questions provided? **Yes**

9. Practical directions for group leaders provided? **Yes**

10. Biblical background for group leaders provided? **No**

11. Biblical background for group members presumed? **No**

12. Participants required to prepare for each session? **No**

Studies Including Both Testaments
Introductions (For Beginners)

INTRODUCTION TO SACRED SCRIPTURE.
Leonard G. Obloy, S.S.L. The Catholic Home Study Institute, 1989. imprimatur. 14 lessons.

This program was devised primarily as a correspondence course for individuals. However, each lesson includes questions for group discussion which enable it to be adapted to group use. This can be done only by arrangement with the Catholic Home Study Institute, which will require that the pastor or a trained person appointed by him correct the assignments (which are usually corrected by the Institute staff) and be available to answer questions during group sessions. If a trained person is not available, an individual could become qualified to lead a group by taking the correspondence course first. The parish coordinator will work under the supervision of the Institute staff.

The minimum cost for a group (up to 23 participants) is $1,500. If there are 24-29 participants, the cost is $60 per person. If there are 50 or more participants, the cost is $50 each. This is far less than it would cost to take this as a correspondence course. Special cost arrangements will be made for parishes under 250 families.

Each participant receives a looseleaf folder with over 500 pages of material, plus the following books: *New American Bible, Recent Discoveries and the Biblical World* and *The Critical Meaning of the Bible* by Raymond Brown, *Mastering the Meaning of the Bible* by John L. McKenzie, *Providentissimus Deus* by Pope Leo XIII, *Divino Afflante Spiritu* by Pope Pius XII, and *Dei Verbum* from the Second Vatican Council.

Each lesson contains reading material planned to take about one hour and a self quiz (answers provided). During the program there are three multiple choice tests and one more extensive test which are to be corrected by the coordinator. Occasionally advanced research/discussion questions are included. All the questions deal with the content presented in the reading material; none of them invites the application of scripture to life.

The basic reading material is by Father Leonard G. Obloy, who received his licentiate in Sacred Scripture from the Pontifical Biblical Institute in Rome and is now a candidate for a doctorate from the same institution. His talks have been broadcast over Vatican Radio.

Topics covered include: inspiration, inerrancy, canonicity, texts and versions, church documents on scripture, hermeneutics, history of biblical interpretation, exegesis, biblical archeology, source criticism, form criticism, redaction criticism, and structural exegesis. Information given is accurate and usually acknowledges the variety of opinions and difficulties in these areas.

This is a very informational approach, with no attempt to lighten the material by illustrations or to connect it to real life situations. The manner of expression will sometimes be difficult for those not accustomed to academics. On the other hand, a great effort is made to define the many technical terms used. The attractive layout includes many such definitions, set off on the page close to where they will be needed.

It would probably not be necessary to have a group session for each of the lessons. The discussion questions for most lessons might well be finished in an hour.

This is an extremely well planned correspondence course, revised on the basis of users' experience. Its goal is to impart correct Roman Catholic teaching about scripture. It is a study <u>about</u> the Bible, not a study <u>of</u> the Bible. It can be adapted to the use of a group if the members want only to gain information without studying the scripture itself or learning to apply it to their lives.

1.	Up-to-date historical critical scholarship incorporated?	Yes
2.	Background information emphasized?	Yes
3.	Application to personal and family life emphasized?	No
4.	Application to the life and mission of the church included?	No
5.	Application to broader social issues included?	No
6.	Sexist language avoided?	No
7.	Guidance for prayer at group meetings provided?	No
8.	Discussion questions provided?	Yes
9.	Practical directions for group leaders provided?	No
10.	Biblical background for group leaders provided?	No
11.	Biblical background for group members presumed?	No
12.	Participants required to prepare for each session?	Yes

Studies Including Both Testaments

Introductions (For Beginners)

PATH THROUGH SCRIPTURE.
Mark Link, S.J. Tabor, 1987. imprimatur. 237 pp., 8 x 10. $10.95. 20 sessions.

Here the popular author Mark Link has risen to the challenge of retelling the entire biblical story in non-technical language, illustrating it with an abundance of brief contemporary stories. Eight chapters cover the Old Testament; 12 the New Testament. Highlights from the Bible itself are included in the Good News translation.

The intent seems to be to provide a text easy to read and attractive to high school students and adults. The format reminds one of *Time Magazine*, with boxes of related information scattered through the main text, and many pictures. Some pictures are of archeological finds or biblical sites; others are of modern teenagers. The style is lively and readable.

Each chapter includes questions to review the content of the chapter, discussion questions on a variety of topics more or less connected with the chapter, suggested activities (sometimes geared to teenagers), suggested additional Bible passages to be read, and suggestions for entries in a prayer journal. A leader would have to plan carefully just how to use this material, and how much preparation to ask participants to do.

The biblical scholarship on which all this is based is somewhat dated, especially in the New Testament section. Perhaps this choice was made to avoid shocking readers with new ideas.

A beginning group wishing a quick and painless overview of the Bible will find this book useful. A leader's guide is also available.

1. Up-to-date historical critical scholarship incorporated?	**Yes**
2. Background information emphasized?	**Yes**
3. Application to personal and family life emphasized?	**Yes**
4. Application to the life and mission of the church included?	**Yes**
5. Application to broader social issues included?	**Yes**
6. Sexist language avoided?	**Yes**

7. Guidance for prayer at group meetings provided?   **No**

8. Discussion questions provided?   **Yes**

9. Practical directions for group leaders provided?   **No**

10. Biblical background for group leaders provided?   **No**

11. Biblical background for group members presumed?   **No**

12. Participants required to prepare for each session?   **Yes**

SCRIPTURE FOUNDATIONS.

Mary Mauren. Scripture Share and Prayer, 1985. 59 pp., 8 ½ x 11, in looseleaf, with four 90 minute audio cassettes. $50. 4 sessions.

This introduction to the Scripture Share and Prayer program does not share the format of the later segments. Participants are not expected to prepare for sessions, and 90 minutes in each of the first three sessions is devoted to input by the leader or by audio tape. Discussion questions follow the input.

The purpose of the first three sessions is to provide overviews of the Old Testament, the New Testament, and the history of the Church. This overview is expected to provide a solid base for future study. It is provided mainly by a "chalk talk" in which the instructor fills in a 12 foot long timeline with simple drawings while giving a very rapid summary of the relevant history. If no instructor is available with courage for such a feat, the tapes can be used while participants follow on a timeline.

Mary Mauren's lively style is well suited to the challenge of such a project. She does particularly well in the Old Testament section, where her enthusiastic recounting of the stories holds the listener's attention. In the New Testament and Church History sections the sheer quantity of information may overwhelm many participants, in spite of the author's skill. Even she sounds breathless sometimes as she rushes through the centuries.

The third session is an overview of church history, including material on revelation. Church history is seen as leading up to Vatican II, and new understandings of the church resulting from Vatican II are emphasized. The Reformation is approached with much ecumenical sensitivity.

The fourth session deals with concepts of God and methods of praying with scripture, especially the Psalms and the *collatio* method. This is an outstanding presentation, and could be used independently of the other three.

It is difficult to imagine a group willing to listen to a 90 minute audio tape tightly packed with information with little emphasis on practical application. However, a group wanting to do this would find these tapes excellent. A teacher wanting to do the "chalk talks" would benefit by listening to the tapes while preparing the presentation. A teacher might also devise ways to spread the material over more than four sessions.

This is a program that requires dedicated and competent leadership. It needs a great deal of careful study by the leader to be well enough understood to be effective.

Handouts are included in the looseleaf notebook with permission to reproduce for members of the group.

The program is available in Spanish for the same price. The first three sessions are also available (in English) on video tape.

See: Scripture Share and Prayer, p.225.

1. Up-to-date historical critical scholarship incorporated? **Yes**

2. Background information emphasized? **Yes**

3. Application to personal and family life emphasized? **Yes**

4. Application to the life and mission of the church included? **Yes**

5. Application to broader social issues included? **No**

6. Sexist language avoided? **Yes**

7. Guidance for prayer at group meetings provided? **Yes**

8. Discussion questions provided? **Yes**

9. Practical directions for group leaders provided? **Yes**

10. Biblical background for group leaders provided? **No**

11. Biblical background for group members presumed? **No**

12. Participants required to prepare for each session? **No**

Studies Including Both Testaments
Introductions (For Beginners)

**WALKING TOGETHER THROUGH THE BIBLE:
AN ORIENTATION COURSE FOR USING
THE CHRISTIAN COMMUNITY BIBLE.**
Robert Delaney. Franciscan Communications, 1989. imprimatur. 32 pp., 5 x 8. $1.25.
6 sessions.

The *Christian Community Bible* was translated and commented on especially for the Christian Communities of the Philippines and the Third World. Franciscan Communications makes it available in the United States. This version contains a unique variety of catechetical aids so that it can serve its purpose for persons who have no access to other books. A casual user would hardly notice many of these features. This orientation course would help beginners develop the skills necessary to get full benefit from using this version of the Bible.

The format is unusual. Each session gives word for word what a leader (called "animator") might say throughout the session. This might be very helpful for a beginning leader to read through as preparation; it would probably be disastrous if the leader used the booklet itself during the session. The booklet suggests that each participant should have a copy, but this is likely to make the session seem very artificial.

The program is geared to participants with no knowledge of the Bible and very limited educational background. Methods emphasized are highlighting of key words, daily memorizing of Bible verses, and much reading aloud of the commentary in the *Christian Community Bible* by volunteers. (The leader may need considerable sensitivity to select readers comfortable in reading aloud and able to do so well enough not to irritate other participants.)

The emphasis is on developing skills needed to use this particular Bible. Some very basic biblical information is also included about Abraham, Moses, Jesus, and the Psalms. No effort is made to introduce the complexities of contemporary scholarship, but participants are taught to read each passage in its context and to use other parts of scripture to illuminate it.

The commentary is quick to connect the biblical stories with contemporary issues. For example, "Moses had been involved earlier in his life with the civil rights conflicts of his people....On one occasion he killed an Egyptian who was beating a Hebrew worker. Moses fled from Egypt. He had suffered `burn-out' in his civil rights activity." Moses removing his sandals at the burning bush is said to teach that "A condition for receiving the gift of conversion is to discard our over-concern with daily affairs." The famous "spoiling of the Egyptians" seems to call for the taxation of the rich in order to rectify the unbalanced distribution of God's creation and to guarantee a "severance pay" for the underprivileged of society.

The questions make similar connections. For example, "Abraham was a man in search for an ideal that was inspired by faith. He felt called to found a better society. Let's apply that to ourselves. The people of the United States are also a people on the move. Fifty per cent of the adults in the USA make some major change every three years--with regard to their work, housing, education, or spouse, etc. What motivates most people to change like this? How can you tell the difference between one person's response in faith to an inner call and another person's restlessness, instability and ambition?"

More sophisticated groups may resent being told how to apply the text instead of being challenged to find out for themselves. But for others, this orientation course may open the riches of the scripture as a living word.

The sexist language which is so conspicuous in the *Christian Community Bible* itself is avoided in the orientation booklet.

Available in Spanish.

1.	Up-to-date historical critical scholarship incorporated?	**No**
2.	Background information emphasized?	**No**
3.	Application to personal and family life emphasized?	**Yes**
4.	Application to the life and mission of the church included?	**Yes**
5.	Application to broader social issues included?	**Yes**
6.	Sexist language avoided?	**Yes**
7.	Guidance for prayer at group meetings provided?	**Yes**
8.	Discussion questions provided?	**Yes**
9.	Practical directions for group leaders provided?	**Yes**
10.	Biblical background for group leaders provided?	**No**
11.	Biblical background for group members presumed?	**No**
12.	Participants required to prepare for each session?	**Yes**

Studies Including Both Testaments

THE BIBLE MAKES SENSE.

Walter Brueggemann. St.Mary's Press, 1977. 155 pp., 5 ¾ x 8. $6.95. 9 sessions.

This book may serve as a good introduction to the work of Walter Brueggemann, who has made a great impact on contemporary biblical studies. Though a professor of Old Testament and thoroughly grounded in contemporary biblical scholarship, Dr. Brueggemann deals with scripture as a whole and in its relationship to the believing community. Scripture is not an answer book, but a partner in an ongoing dialogue with believers about their lives. It witnesses to faithful relationships able to energize and challenge the church today. If taken seriously, it will turn our world upside down and lead us in ever new paths.

This is not a book for beginners. The author assumes a knowledge of biblical history, geography, and literature, and moves beyond this to a new synthesis. He aims to make readers "insiders" to the biblical world by cultivating in them a "historical imagination" which gives biblical history a dynamism that impacts contemporary situations. He deals in fresh ways with a variety of biblical themes, making bold connections between the Old and New Testaments.

For Brueggemann, the Bible is not a closed book but opens into the life of the church. For example, he lists four cases of renewal based on return to the written word: King Josiah, Luther, Wesley, and Vatican II. (This is also an example of the very ecumenical approach of this Protestant scholar.)

Each chapter is followed by suggestions of two to four brief scripture passages for meditation and about three questions for reflection and discussion. These are challenging questions, calling participants to connect the ideas in the book with their personal experiences. Not all groups will be ready for the deep personal sharing called for. Some will need more or different questions.

Since there is no strong continuity from chapter to chapter, persons who do not attend regularly should be able to participate as long as they read the chapter for the session they do attend. Chapter 10 is a very fine summary of the book, but it does not have reflection and discussion questions or suggested scripture readings.

For a sophisticated, well educated group, this is a challenging and enriching book.

1. Up-to-date historical critical scholarship incorporated?   **Yes**

2. Background information emphasized?   **Yes**

3. Application to personal and family life emphasized?   **Yes**

4. Application to the life and mission of the church included?   **Yes**

5. Application to broader social issues included?   **Yes**

6. Sexist language avoided?   **Yes**

7. Guidance for prayer at group meetings provided?   **No**

8. Discussion questions provided?   **Yes**

9. Practical directions for group leaders provided?   **No**

10. Biblical background for group leaders provided?   **No**

11. Biblical background for group members presumed?   **Yes**

12. Participants required to prepare for each session?   **Yes**

Studies Including Both Testaments

* COME, FOLLOW ME.

Donald Senior, C.P. Treehaus Communications, 1986. 4 videotapes, 30 minutes each, with Viewer Guide and copy of script. $199.80. 8 sessions.

These eight video segments (two per tape) are exceptionally powerful. The audio portion consists of very moving reflections by Father Senior on:

> The Desert: Place of New Beginnings
> Bethlehem and Nazareth: God's Unexpected Ways
> Jerusalem: Search for Unity
> Way of the Passion: The Cause of Justice
> Capernaum and the Sea: The Risks of Discipleship
> Jericho: Jesus, Oasis for Outcasts
> Caesarea Maritima: The Universal Mission of the Church
> The Mountains: Vision of Who Jesus Is.

Beginning with some aspect of the Holy Land, each reflection traces a theme through scripture and applies it in very practical ways to contemporary life. Father Senior's grasp of the relevant scholarship is so profound that he is able to utilize it in bringing the scripture to life without a touch of the pedantic. His pastoral sense is such that he speaks directly to where ordinary people live.

The video portion consists primarily in lively and beautiful scenes from the Holy Land with Father Senior appearing occasionally in the scene. Interspersed are scenes from contemporary life in the United States and in many other parts of the world skillfully tied into the message being spoken. This is an outstanding use of the video tape medium.

This program is unique in its appeal to people of varied ages and levels of biblical knowledge. A biblical scholar could be moved by the evocative visuals, and a person with no biblical knowledge whatever could appreciate the reflections.

The video tapes are accompanied by a copy of the text of all the reflections, a list of scripture passages to be read for each segment, reflection questions, discussion questions and activities, and recommendations for group leaders.

Group leaders would need to preview each tape and plan the sessions according to the needs of their particular group. A group willing to do the scripture readings in advance might need time to discuss their reading before viewing the video. A group that comes unprepared could still benefit from the video and utilize the discussion questions. The material could be adapted for groups meeting for from half an hour to two hours. (A two-hour session would probably use two segments.) It is highly recommended that groups who can do so view the segment, take some silent reflection time, discuss the suggested questions, and end by a second viewing. There is more in each video than can be grasped at one viewing.

Segments can be used in many settings other than discussion groups: liturgies, classrooms, private viewing, family prayer, preparation of pilgrims going to the Holy Land, etc. If they are fully utilized, they should be a good investment for any parish.

This is an outstanding resource for groups looking for a reflective, right brain, approach to the Bible. For groups wanting to do a more traditional type of study, it will add a valuable dimension if used occasionally in conjunction with other materials.

1. Up-to-date historicalcritical scholarship incorporated? **Yes**

2. Background information emphasized? **No**

3. Application to personal and family life emphasized? **Yes**

4. Application to the life and mission of the church included? **Yes**

5. Application to broader social issues included? **Yes**

6. Sexist language avoided? **Yes**

7. Guidance for prayer at group meetings provided? **No**

8. Discussion questions provided? **Yes**

9. Practical directions for group leaders provided? **Yes**

10. Biblical background for group leaders provided? **No**

11. Biblical background for group members presumed? **No**

12. Participants required to prepare for each session? **No**

Studies Including Both Testaments
General Studies

SEASONS OF FAITH: ADULT WORKBOOK, CYCLE B: BACKGROUND FOR THE SUNDAY LECTIONARY.
Brown, 1991. imprimatur. 130 pp., 8 ½ x 11. $7.95. 52 sessions.

This book consists in one tear out sheet (2 sides) for each Sunday. One side of the sheet lists the scripture readings for the Sunday and gives background for them. The other side contains questions for discussion, starters for journaling, and blank space for the journaling.

The commentary begins with a paragraph evoking some common experience related to the day's theme, then gives a series of bits of information which provide background for one or other of the readings. The background comes from biblical scholarship or liturgy. Occasionally this would make little sense to a person who had done no biblical study (who, for instance did not know about the sources of the Pentateuch or the exile or Second Isaiah). However, the background information might be useful to someone preparing a homily, or preparing to lead a discussion on the Sunday readings. Some leaders may prefer to read the commentary privately and use or adapt the discussion questions without group members having copies of the book.

The discussion questions do not deal with the scripture texts in detail, but challenge participants to apply them to a wide variety of issues. Some deal with the theme rather than specifically with the scripture texts. The questions tend to surface personal experience. Some call for a depth of personal sharing which may not be comfortable for all. The questions do not assume that the commentary has been read.

The "journal starters" are generally sentences to be completed. For example, "I am a light for the world when...," "I am like Peter when I ...," "God has surprised me by..."

It is not altogether clear how this book is intended to be used, but it does offer resources for a group studying the weekly readings. Formats might be devised for brief sessions or longer ones, with or without preparation by participants.

Cycle B is read in 1993-94 and 1996-97. Similar books for Cycles A and C will be available.

1.	Up-to-date historical critical scholarship incorporated?	**Yes**
2.	Background information emphasized?	**Yes**
3.	Application to personal and family life emphasized?	**Yes**

---

4. Application to the life and mission of the church included?   **Yes**

5. Application to broader social issues included?   **Yes**

6. Sexist language avoided?   **Yes**

7. Guidance for prayer at group meetings provided?   **No**

8. Discussion questions provided?   **Yes**

9. Practical directions for group leaders provided?   **No**

10. Biblical background for group leaders provided?   **No**

11. Biblical background for group members presumed?   **Yes**

12. Participants required to prepare for each session?   **No**

Studies Including Both Testaments

General Studies

UNEXPECTED NEWS: READING THE BIBLE WITH THIRD WORLD EYES.

Robert McAfee Brown. Westminster Press, 1984. 166 pp., 5 ¼ x 8. $9.00. 10 sessions.

This book looks at ten familiar Bible stories through new eyes, the eyes of the oppressed people of Latin America. It make us aware that when third world Christians listen to the Bible, they hear different things than we do. They notice that the God of the Bible sides with the oppressed, which means to them that God sides with them and therefore against those (such as citizens of the United States) who grow rich from oppression. This is an unsettling book, which aims to be provocative rather than balanced.

Dr. Brown is not unaware of contemporary biblical scholarship, but he writes with the "second naivete" of those who, after all the academic work is done, return to the biblical story to see what it has to say for life today.

Inclusive language is used even at the cost of altering scripture quotations.

Each chapter ends with "Items for reflection and discussion." These are not the typical open-ended "discussion questions" provided in books for Bible study groups. They call for the application of scripture to contemporary issues in controversial ways that will stir up lively discussion in most groups. Sometimes they are in the form of "thought starters" such as contemporary versions of biblical stories. For example, the parable Nathan told to David is retold as the story of a corporate executive who turns a nation of tiny farms into a vast coffee plantation, depriving the poor farmers of their whole livelihood in order to increase his vast wealth. In another chapter, after the story of the lawyer who summarizes the law as love of God and neighbor to Jesus' approval, this question is asked: "What do Jesus' question and the lawyer's answer suggest about being neighbors today in relation to: a) legislation to protect the rights of minority groups, b) the diminution of social services for the poor, and c) the Unites States' manipulation of the destinies of small nations in Central America?"

A bibliography is included, which lists Latin American and North American works.

This book will lead to exciting discussions for groups open to the social justice dimension of scripture, whether or not they have background in biblical study.

1. Up-to-date historical critical scholarship incorporated?   **Yes**

2. Background information emphasized?   **No**

3. Application to personal and family life emphasized?   **No**

4. Application to the life and mission of the church included?   **Yes**

5. Application to broader social issues included?   **Yes**

6. Sexist language avoided?   **Yes**

7. Guidance for prayer at group meetings provided?   **No**

8. Discussion questions provided?   **Yes**

9. Practical directions for group leaders provided?   **No**

10. Biblical background for group leaders provided?   **No**

11. Biblical background for group members presumed?   **No**

12. Participants required to prepare for each session?   **Yes**

* COME, HOLY SPIRIT, RENEW THE WHOLE CREATION.
Friendship Press, 1989. 94 pp., 6 x 9. $4.95. 6 sessions.

This unique program was developed in preparation for the Seventh Assembly of the World Council of Churches. However, the message of the Christians throughout the world who speak in this book is in no way outdated.

Each study is based on three passages, one each from the Old Testament, the Gospel, and other New Testament writings. The principal texts studied are: the Pentecost story, the Magnificat, the first creation story, Isaiah 61:1-4 (anointed to preach the good news), 1 Cor 12:1-13:3 (gifts of the Holy Spirit), and the Baptism of Jesus.

After about three pages of explanation of the passage being studied, there are three to five pages of brief reflections on the passage by Christians from many parts of the world. The power of this book is in the enrichment brought to the biblical text by seeing it from the perspective of many different cultures, especially cultures of developing countries.

Brief opening and closing prayers and discussion questions are also provided. The questions encourage global application of the text, with emphasis on oppressed peoples and ecology.

This book is also suitable for private reading. It is a powerful word of hope in the power of the Holy Spirit to renew the whole creation.

1.	Up-to-date historical critical scholarship incorporated?	**Yes**
2.	Background information emphasized?	**No**
3.	Application to personal and family life emphasized?	**No**
4.	Application to the life and mission of the church included?	**Yes**
5.	Application to broader social issues included?	**Yes**
6.	Sexist language avoided?	**Yes**
7.	Guidance for prayer at group meetings provided?	**Yes**
8.	Discussion questions provided?	**Yes**
9.	Practical directions for group leaders provided?	**No**

10. Biblical background for group leaders provided?   **No**

11. Biblical background for group members presumed?   **No**

12. Participants required to prepare for each session?   **Yes**

HARPER'S NEW AMERICAN BIBLE STUDY PROGRAM.
Harper and Row, San Francisco, 1990. Administrative Guide: 78 pp., 7 ½ x 9. $19.95. Leader's Guide: 274 pp., 7 ½ x 9. $24.95. Resource Book (for each participant) 230 pp., 7 ½ x 9. $19.95. 33 or more sessions.

This program, developed by the Presbyterians in the '70s under the title "Kerygma" has been updated and revised for Catholic use. It studies ten themes: God saves the people; God is faithful to the people; God's people reflect on God; People live in God's world; God's people have leaders; God's people have kings and a king; God's law demands a righteous people; God's people learn wisdom; God's people worship; God's people have hope. Each theme is traced through the Old and New Testaments. The best in contemporary biblical scholarship and adult educational methodology underlies the program.

Before the ten themes there are three introductory chapters on the canon, translations, and tools for biblical study. The participants' reading for these sessions is so dense even the brave might become discouraged. Leaders may want to omit some of these chapters, or encourage participants by assuring them that it does get more interesting at the fourth session. One stated goal is to make the Bible come alive in the context of the church, which leads to a heavy emphasis on the relationship between Bible and church, and Bible and liturgy. The editing for Catholic use seems to have been very thorough since reference is always to the Catholic church.

Another goal is to give an experience of the Bible as a whole. Each session is based on a number of short passages from different parts of the Bible. The themes are seen as a way of making connections between books of the Bible. This is an excellent method for people already acquainted with most of the individual books, but it could well be overwhelming for one who begins biblically illiterate.

The Administrative Guide contains helpful suggestions about how this program should be integrated into the overall program of a parish. Parish planners would benefit from reading this carefully before making definite plans. Otherwise they may start scheduling and recruiting without being aware of the variety of ways in which this program can be offered. For instance, the Guide informs them that what appears to be 33 sessions is actually more effective if expanded into 45 or 50 sessions. Information about the type of leaders and participants which the program assumes is also important. The Administrative Guide contains many tips useful in any adult education situation. It supports the principles behind the program from Catholic church documents.

The Leader's Guide in its preface repeats some of the information in the Administrative Guide. (If you decide not to invest in the Administrative Guide, be sure to read this preface carefully before setting the program up.) The Leader's Guide is the best part of the program. It provides for each session background biblical information and references for study, and a fine variety of options for learning activities. spite of the claim of the program that leaders do not need special training, th reviewer believes that the program can only be effective with leaders with so biblical background, good adult education skills, and several hours to prepare ea session. The leader is not expected to lecture, but because of the widely scattere passages studied in each session, many more questions are likely to arise than a answered in the Leader's Guide or the Resource Book. If the leader is not a biblic resource person, a group might end up feeling they had been exposed to a long stri of disconnected, out of context quotations which led to more questions than insigh Team leadership is recommended, so that the leaders can take turns assumir primary responsibility for the themes. This could reduce the preparation time fo leaders to a more practical amount.

Each participant needs a Resource Book. This provides in an attractive format the li of passages to be read for each session, about four pages of helpful backgrour material about those passages, suggestions for further study, and questions fo reflection. An appendix includes a timeline, maps, pronunciation guide, and list translations (unfortunately not up to date). By following the symbols explained in th preface, a participant can tell the relative importance of the many quotations referre to, and do whatever time permits. What each one gets from the program will deper mainly on the quantity and quality of time put into preparation. Two to four hou each week are recommended. Ninety percent of this is spent on the scripture itse Individuals not committed to regular study and attendance are not likely to get mu from this program.

Groups not willing to commit to 33 weeks can use the material in shorter segmen For individuals who have already studied many books of the Bible, this is an ide way to review and tie together. For beginners, it might seem to be very hard wo leading to a quick once-through but lacking in depth.

1.	Up-to-date historical critical scholarship incorporated?	Yes
2.	Background information emphasized?	Yes
3.	Application to personal and family life emphasized?	Yes
4.	Application to the life and mission of the church included?	Yes
5.	Application to broader social issues included?	Yes
6.	Sexist language avoided?	Yes
7.	Guidance for prayer at group meetings provided?	Yes
8.	Discussion questions provided?	Yes
9.	Practical directions for group leaders provided?	Yes
10.	Biblical background for group leaders provided?	Yes
11.	Biblical background for group members presumed?	Yes
12.	Participants required to prepare for each session?	Yes

NTERPRETING SCRIPTURE:
CATHOLIC RESPONSE TO FUNDAMENTALISM.

Iwin Daschbach, S.V.D. Brown, 1985. imprimatur. 124 pp. 6 x 8. $6.95. 8 sessions.

Catholic priest with long experience in the Bible Belt provides information intrasting the fundamentalist and contextualist approaches to scripture. A reader acquainted with contemporary biblical scholarship might be overwhelmed by his pid listing of old ideas about the Bible which modern scholarship has questioned. e nature of the book does not allow time to sort out which of the scholarly views e generally accepted and which more controversial. Nor is there time to show the ositive spiritual value of the scholarly discoveries. This is a crash course on areas conflict between Catholics and others: divorce, original sin, the rapture, millennium, anti-Christ, etc.

ost groups would probably prefer to learn the contrast between the two approaches more gradually, while they focused on the Bible itself and its message for eir lives. This book, which offers information rather than inspiration, might serve a reference when questions arise, rather than as the basis for discussion.

cause of the heavy reliance on Roman Catholic church documents, this book will most useful to Roman Catholics and others interested in knowing the Catholic sition on scripture. Father Daschbach says, correctly, that the Catholic position not different from that of other mainline groups, but he does not quote documents om other sources.

iscussion questions are provided for each of the eight chapters, and groups which ave already been introduced to the Bible and wish to focus on issues of Catholic-ndamentalist conflict for eight sessions might find this book a helpful basis for iscussion. Recommended for advanced groups primarily concerned with understanding the difference between Catholic and fundamentalist approaches to the ble.

1. Up-to-date historical critical scholarship incorporated? **Yes**

2. Background information emphasized? **Yes**

3. Application to personal and family life emphasized? **No**

4. Application to the life and mission of the church included? **No**

5. Application to broader social issues included? **No**

6. Sexist language avoided?   **Yes**

7. Guidance for prayer at group meetings provided?   **No**

8. Discussion questions provided?   **Yes**

9. Practical directions for group leaders provided?   **No**

10. Biblical background for group leaders provided?   **No**

11. Biblical background for group members presumed?   **Yes**

12. Participants required to prepare for each session?   **Yes**

Studies Including Both Testaments

JOURNEYING IN HIS LIGHT.

William A. Anderson, D.Min. Brown, 1987. 179 pp., 6 x 9. $6.50. 37 sessions.

This book can be adapted for a variety of uses: as companion to *In His Light* for RCIA, for youth, high school, adult or family groups, private prayer, etc. In any case, it aims at prayerful reflection on participants' lives in the light of scripture, not at study.

Each session deals with a theme such as: The Wonders of Love, In Search of God, Knowing God Better, Jesus Is Lord, Sin and Life, Baptism, Confirmation, Eucharist, Reconciliation, Marriage, Anointing of the Sick, the liturgy for the weeks of Lent and Holy Week. These can be used in any order, and can be used separately from each other. Reflections on the Lenten readings offer options for years A, B, and C and might well be used by groups meeting during Lent only. Members could then use the Holy Week reflections privately.

Each session contains an introductory story or reflection from life, three scripture references (each with a reflection and a question), space for personal response, three questions for discussion, and a brief closing prayer which flows out of the material read. The discussion questions call for sharing on the theme out of personal experience; they do not usually deal with scripture.

This is a very nonthreatening program for Catholics or catechumens interested in growing in their spiritual lives.

1.	Incorporates up-to-date historical critical scholarship.	**No**
2.	Background information emphasized?	**No**
3.	Application to personal and family life emphasized?	**Yes**
4.	Application to the life and mission of the church included?	**Yes**
5.	Application to broader social issues included?	**No**
6.	Sexist language avoided?	**Yes**
7.	Guidance for prayer at group meetings provided?	**Yes**
8.	Discussion questions provided?	**Yes**
9.	Practical directions for group leaders provided?	**No**

10. Biblical background for group leaders provided?　　**No**

11. Biblical background for group members presumed?　　**No**

12. Participants required to prepare for each session?　　**Yes**

OVE AND JUSTICE: A BIBLICAL UNDERSTANDING.

a O'Dian. Covenant Bible Studies. Brethren Press, 1990. 40 pp., 5 ½ x 8 ½. $2.95. 10 ssions.

ie goal of this program is to help the participant to look in new ways at the biblical ncepts of justice and love, at the system of justice in our country, and at our rsonal responses to God's call to do justice. The author, who has personal perience of prison ministry, is particularly effective at picturing vividly the justices of our present "justice system."

ich lesson is based on a few verses of scripture. Some questions call for study of ese and comparison with other parts of scripture. However, the majority of the iestions for preparation and also those for discussion deal with current issues and ays to become constructively involved in them.

ich chapter, as throughout this series, consists in three and a half pages of input, lus questions. The input includes some good scriptural insights, many contempo- ry stories from the author's experience, and factual and theological arguments ;ainst present policies toward the poor and those accused of crime. This is an oquent call for radical Christian living, aimed at the "Peaceable Kingdom" or "The pside Down World."

ee: **Covenant Bible Studies, p.209.**

1.	Up-to-date historical critical scholarship incorporated?	**Yes**
2.	Background information emphasized?	**No**
3.	Application to personal and family life emphasized?	**Yes**
4.	Application to the life and mission of the church included?	**Yes**
5.	Application to broader social issues included?	**Yes**
6.	Sexist language avoided?	**Yes**
7.	Guidance for prayer at group meetings provided?	**No**
8.	Discussion questions provided?	**Yes**
9.	Practical directions for group leaders provided?	**No**

10. Biblical background for group leaders provided?   **No**

11. Biblical background for group members presumed?   **No**

12. Participants required to prepare for each session?   **Yes**

PEACEMAKING.

lary Schramm. Small-Group Bible Study. Augsburg, 1986. 32 pp., 5 ½ x 8 ¼. $1.20.
sessions.

his is a Bible study liable to change participants' lives and attitudes. A wide range
f brief passages from throughout the Bible are assigned to be read. Questions ask
e participant to apply these passages to personal, family, congregational, and
ational issues. Racism, the environment, and global economic imbalance are all
rought into the discussion. Occasionally a series of common opinions are listed and
articipants are asked if they agree, disagree, or have no opinion. In a group with
ixed opinions very lively discussion is to be expected.

his is a very well designed program to explore the biblical word on peacemaking
nd possibilities for applying it in the modern world. Participants need to spend
rayerful time in preparation looking up the many passages and reflecting on their
pplication. With that preparation and the service of a good facilitator, this program
 practically guaranteed to be a soul-shaking experience. It uncovers an often
verlooked challenge of the gospel.

ee: **Small-Group Bible Study, p.227.**

1.	Incorporates up-to-date historical critical scholarship.	**No**
2.	Background information emphasized?	**No**
3.	Application to personal and family life emphasized?	**Yes**
4.	Application to the life and mission of the church included?	**Yes**
5.	Application to broader social issues included?	**Yes**
6.	Sexist language avoided?	**Yes**
7.	Guidance for prayer at group meetings provided?	**Yes**
8.	Discussion questions provided?	**Yes**
9.	Practical directions for group leaders provided?	**No**
10.	Biblical background for group leaders provided?	**No**
11.	Biblical background for group members presumed?	**No**
12.	Participants required to prepare for each session?	**Yes**

ECOVERY FROM DISTORTED IMAGES OF GOD.

ͦale and Juanita Ryan. Life Recovery Guides. Intervarsity Press, 1990. 59 pp.,
½ x 8. $3.95. 6 sessions.

ƭhis program aims to enable people struggling for wholeness to hear the Good News.
 addresses one of the burdens borne by many hurting people: distorted images of
ͦod, most often developed because of dysfunctional family situations. Images
ͭudied are: The God of Impossible Expectations, The Emotionally Distant God, The
ͽisinterested God, The Abusive God, The Unreliable God, and The God Who
ͤbandons.

ƭhe introduction states, "...these studies are rooted in the conviction that the Bible
ͤn be a significant resource for recovery. Many people who have lived through
ͺfficult life experiences have had bits of the Bible thrown at their pain as a quick fix
ͬ a simplistic solution. As a result, many people expect the Bible to be a barrier to
ͺcovery rather than a resource. These studies are based on the belief that the Bible
 not a book of quick fixes and simplistic solutions. It is, on the contrary, a practical
ͷd helpful resource for recovery."

ͤach session begins with one page explaining how a particular distorted image of
ͦod is related to some childhood deprivation. This explanation is to be read aloud
ͷ the group. Following are questions in workbook format about relevant experi-
ͷces of the participant. Then a passage from scripture is to be read aloud, followed
ͽ another series of questions based on the scripture passage which help participants
ͽe how contrary the image of God scripture presents is to the distorted image. Brief
ͽuided meditations are sometimes also given.

ͷnswers to all the questions are to be written in the workbook, either during quiet
ͷmes within the session or beforehand. These questions are likely to lead to
ͬofound sharing of personal pain, but the leader's instructions insist that persons
ͺe to share only what they feel comfortable sharing.

ͷhis program is aimed at people of any denomination or none. No knowledge of the
ͺble or church teaching is presumed. One would not even have to own a Bible, since
ͺe passages on which the studies are based are presented in the booklet. However,
ͭher scriptural passages for further reading are sometimes suggested.

ͷhile the emphasis is certainly more on personal growth than on learning about the
ͺble, some interesting insights arise from using the deeply hurtful experiences of life
 a tool for interpreting scripture. For example, when the Pharisees mutter among
ͷemselves against Jesus instead of speaking directly to him, it is suggested that this

style of communication will be familiar to many who grew up in dysfunction families.

In the back of the book very practical suggestions are given for the leader abou handling possible problems, scriptural or concerning group dynamics, which mig arise for each question discussed.

The introduction emphasizes that the program is intended as an enrichment for recovery program or for professional counseling, not a substitute for either. Thoug the booklet is designed for group use, it includes suggestions for adapting it fc individual use.

This is a very well designed program responding to a very real need.

1.	Up-to-date historical critical scholarship incorporated?	No
2.	Background information emphasized?	No
3.	Application to personal and family life emphasized?	Yes
4.	Application to the life and mission of the church included?	No
5.	Application to broader social issues included?	No
6.	Sexist language avoided?	No
7.	Guidance for prayer at group meetings provided?	Yes
8.	Discussion questions provided?	Yes
9.	Practical directions for group leaders provided?	Yes
10.	Biblical background for group leaders provided?	No
11.	Biblical background for group members presumed?	No
12.	Participants required to prepare for each session?	No

BIBLICAL WOMAN:
CONTEMPORARY FEMINIST REFLECTIONS
ON SCRIPTURAL TEXTS.
Denise Lardner Carmody. Crossroad, 1988. 144 pp., 5 ½ x 8. $10.95. 12 or 24 sessions.

Brief scripture passages about women are used as starting points for 24 reflections. Contemporary biblical scholarship is utilized, as well as a smattering of anthropology, church history, Catholic, Protestant and Jewish writings, and feminist literature. The purpose is to engage feminists in a dialogue with the Bible, emphasizing the support they can find there but not denying the problems.

Each reflection ends with three discussion questions which could be used by groups. Many groups might prefer to read and discuss two of the reflections (5-7 pages each) for each session. The verse or two dealt with directly is printed at the beginning of each reflection, but often makes little sense by itself. A leader interested in scripture might want to look for the context of that passage and assign the entire passage for preparation. For a group with excellent scripture background, the book could be used as it stands as a basis for discussing the Bible's varied messages about women. Recommended for well educated groups concerned about feminist issues.

1.	Incorporates up-to-date historical critical scholarship.	**Yes**
2.	Background information emphasized?	**Yes**
3.	Application to personal and family life emphasized?	**Yes**
4.	Application to the life and mission of the church included?	**Yes**
5.	Application to broader social issues included?	**Yes**
6.	Sexist language avoided?	**Yes**
7.	Guidance for prayer at group meetings provided?	**No**
8.	Discussion questions provided?	**Yes**
9.	Practical directions for group leaders provided?	**No**
10.	Biblical background for group leaders provided?	**No**
11.	Biblical background for group members presumed?	**No**
12.	Participants required to prepare for each session?	**Yes**

GOD OF OUR MOTHERS:
SEVEN BIBLICAL WOMEN TELL THEIR STORIES.
Martha Ann Kirk, C.C.V.I. St. Anthony Messenger Press, 1985. 2 audio tapes with discussion guide included. $16.95. 8 sessions.

This is an extremely effective resource for groups wishing to reflect imaginatively on the women of the Bible and to find in their lives insights for today.

Each tape consists of four segments of about 15 minutes each. In the first segment Sister Martha Ann Kirk speaks of the importance of women's stories and of her method of entering creatively into the biblical text to uncover the stories of women which are not seen as important by the male authors. In the remaining seven segments biblical women tell their own stories: Sarah, Hagar, Miriam, Ruth, Susanna, Mary of Magdala, and Martha. These are dramatic monologues, well presented by a variety of readers. We hear Sarah's feelings as she waited for the return of Abraham and Isaac from Mount Moriah, Hagar's homesickness for her native Egypt when she was a young slave in Abraham's tent, Martha's response to Jesus' words to her (which led him and Mary to help her peel the vegetables), and many other things the biblical authors neglected to tell us.

All of this is highly entertaining, but it is much more. Those knowledgeable in biblical scholarship will see that the stories are based on the best information available, though the scholarly background is never mentioned. And those concerned about women's issues will appreciate the sensitive way in which the experience of biblical women is told in the light of our awareness of the experience of single mothers, rape victims, widows, poor elderly women, women involved in church ministry, and so forth. As the introduction says so aptly, "we 'overhear' our own story in the stories of Scripture."

The guide which comes with the tapes provides everything that is needed to use the tapes as the basis for eight group sessions. The scripture text on which the story is based is indicated first. Ideally, it should be read before the session. Scripture and other reading suggestions are also given for after the session. A form for sharing prayer at the beginning and end of sessions and suggestions for journaling are also provided. Most valuable are the questions for discussion and reflection.

This reviewer has experienced the remarkable response evoked by these tapes, especially in groups of women. They easily elicit the sharing of personal experience, and lead even women who would vigorously reject the title "feminist" to grow in their sensitivity to women's issues.

The tapes are also suitable for private listening and reflection, and the guide suggests a variety of settings in which particular segments can be used, e.g. Hagar with abuse spouses or single parents, Miriam on Holy Saturday or for child protection programs, Ruth for widows or intergenerational programs, Susanna for support victims of sexual violence. This is a unique educational tool for many purpose Language used is sensitive to feminist concerns and avoids masculine pronouns for God.

1.	Incorporates up-to-date historical critical scholarship.	**No**
2.	Background information emphasized?	**No**
3.	Application to personal and family life emphasized?	**Yes**
4.	Application to the life and mission of the church included?	**Yes**
5.	Application to broader social issues included?	**Yes**
6.	Sexist language avoided?	**Yes**
7.	Guidance for prayer at group meetings provided?	**Yes**
8.	Discussion questions provided?	**Yes**
9.	Practical directions for group leaders provided?	**Yes**
10.	Biblical background for group leaders provided?	**No**
11.	Biblical background for group members presumed?	**No**
12.	Participants required to prepare for each session?	**No**

WOMEN, MEN, AND THE BIBLE.

Virginia Ramey Mollenkott. Crossroad, 1989. 163 pp., 8 x 5 ¼. $9.95. 7 sessions.

This is an easily understood introduction to some basic concerns of Christian feminism written by a professor of English acquainted with biblical scholarship. While her conservative Protestant background shows at times, it does not detract from the value of the book for those of other traditions. Mollenkott's main concern is to describe and argue against Christian writings which claim that women should be subservient to their husbands. She argues instead that the New Testament teaches mutual submissiveness. She deals with many Old and New Testament passages concerning women but emphasizes the Pauline passages.

A Study Guide is included with exercises to be done in a group or alone before reading each chapter. These involve careful analysis of short scripture passages showing that they are often more favorable to women's causes than is generally realized.

1.	Up-to-date historical critical scholarship incorporated?	**Yes**
2.	Background information emphasized?	**Yes**
3.	Application to personal and family life emphasized?	**Yes**
4.	Application to the life and mission of the church included?	**Yes**
5.	Application to broader social issues included?	**Yes**
6.	Sexist language avoided?	**Yes**
7.	Guidance for prayer at group meetings provided?	**No**
8.	Discussion questions provided?	**Yes**
9.	Practical directions for group leaders provided?	**Yes**
10.	Biblical background for group leaders provided?	**No**
11.	Biblical background for group members presumed?	**No**
12.	Participants required to prepare for each session?	**No**

Reviews of Individual Programs

Section II:
Old Testament

Old Testament

* BLESSED BY THE GOD OF
ABRAHAM, ISAAC, AND JACOB.

Bless Bible Studies for residents of health care centers and nursing homes. Augsburg, 1988. Participant Book: 24 pp., 8 ¼ x 11. $2.70. Leader Guide: 48 pp., 8 ¼ x 11. $6.40. 12 sessions.

For each session, a familiar story from the Old Testament leads into discussion on one of these themes: Caring for Others (creation story), Listening to God (Noah), The Friend of God (Abraham), Waiting for God (Abraham and Sarah), Wrestling with God (Jacob), Favoritism (Joseph), Forgiveness (Joseph), Laws for Our Lives (Moses), Family Loyalty (Ruth), Strength (David and Goliath), Hope in the Valley (Ezekiel's vision of dry bones), Risk-taking (Esther). An excellent program for its purpose.

See: Bless Bible Studies, p. 207.

1.	Incorporates up-to-date historical critical scholarship.	No
2.	Background information emphasized?	No
3.	Application to personal and family life emphasized?	Yes
4.	Application to the life and mission of the church included?	No
5.	Application to broader social issues included?	Yes
6.	Sexist language avoided?	Yes
7.	Guidance for prayer at group meetings provided?	Yes
8.	Discussion questions provided?	Yes
9.	Practical directions for group leaders provided?	Yes
10.	Biblical background for group leaders provided?	No
11.	Biblical background for group members presumed?	No
12.	Participants required to prepare for each session?	No

Old Testament

A GUIDE TO READING THE OLD TESTAMENT: PART ONE - GOD BEGINS.

ACTA Publications, 1986 (revised edition). imprimatur. 95 pp., 8 ½ x 5 ¼. $2.50.
8 sessions.

Eight sessions introduce: Abraham, Moses, Joshua, David, Amos, and the creation account. The presentations are based on historical critical scholarship, though occasional details might be argued. The chapters are connected to present a fair overview of Old Testament history up to the division of the monarchy.

Each session gives a brief introduction, a list of several chapters of scripture to be read, some helpful background information, connections with the New Testament and Catholic tradition, questions to serve as review of material read with space for writing in answers, and other questions suitable for discussion. Illustrations, maps, and charts contribute to an attractive format.

The background material given is so brief that many problems raised by the chapters being read are not touched. It would be desirable to have a resource person in the group able to answer such questions, or at least some good reference books. The consistent effort to connect scripture with Catholic teaching, liturgy, tradition and experience is a unique asset of this program.

The method is practical and the material easily understood. This would be a good program for a Catholic group with no knowledge of the Old Testament which wished to look briefly at its highpoints and spend some discussion time applying it to their own lives. Available in Spanish.

See: A Guide to Reading the Old Testament: Part Two, p. 69
    A Guide to Reading the New Testament: Part One, p. 109

1. Incorporates up-to-date historical critical scholarship.   Yes

2. Background information emphasized?   Yes

3. Application to personal and family life emphasized?   Yes

4. Application to the life and mission of the church included?   Yes

5. Application to broader social issues included?   Yes

6. Sexist language avoided?   No

7. Guidance for prayer at group meetings provided? **No**

8. Discussion questions provided? **Yes**

9. Practical directions for group leaders provided? **No**

10. Biblical background for group leaders provided? **No**

11. Biblical background for group members presumed? **No**

12. Participants required to prepare for each session? **Yes**

A GUIDE TO READING THE OLD TESTAMENT: PART TWO - THE STAGE IS SET.

ACTA Publications. 1986 (revised edition). imprimatur. 96 pp., 5 ¼ x 8 ½. $2.50. sessions.

Another eight sessions continue the same methodology as Part One into the later part of Old Testament history. The chapters treat: Psalms, Isaiah, Ezekiel, the restoration, Ruth, Jonah, Job, the Maccabees, and Daniel. Available in Spanish.

See: A Guide to Reading the Old Testament: Part One, p. 67
     A Guide to Reading the New Testament, Part One, p. 109

1.	Up-to-date historical critical scholarship incorporated?	Yes
2.	Background information emphasized?	Yes
3.	Application to personal and family life emphasized?	Yes
4.	Application to the life and mission of the church included?	Yes
5.	Application to broader social issues included?	Yes
6.	Sexist language avoided?	No
7.	Guidance for prayer at group meetings provided?	No
8.	Discussion questions provided?	Yes
9.	Practical directions for group leaders provided?	No
10.	Biblical background for group leaders provided?	No
11.	Biblical background for group members presumed?	No
12.	Participants required to prepare for each session?	Yes

JONAH AND RUTH.

James Limburg. Friendship Bible Study Series. Augsburg Press, 1989. Study Book, 48 pp., 5 ½ x 8 ½. $2.85. Leader's Guide, 32 pp., 5 ½ x 8 ½. $3.10. 8 sessions.

This is an easy going Bible study for one hour sessions for church or ecumenical groups. It will be appreciated especially by groups where neither leader nor members have done or want to do the more academic type of biblical study. Emphasis is on reading these two stories carefully as stories and finding their application for Christian living today.

Sensitive comments and questions bring out the gentle message of Ruth for family and community life and the challenge of Jonah toward global awareness and ecological issues (even the animals fast). Participants also note how unobtrusively God works in Ruth, and how obtrusively in Jonah. All of this in a light vein with emphasis on the friendships being fostered among members of the study group.

If a question arises as to whether Jonah is fact or fiction, the leader is advised to refuse to deal with it until the entire story has been read and discussed. One of the questions for reflection for the last lesson is "The Bible contains a variety of types of literature, such as historical writing (2 Kings 17:1-6, reporting the fall of Sumaria), fable (Judges 9:7-15, where trees talk to one another), proverb (Proverbs 10) and parable (Isaiah 5:1-7; Luke 10:25-37). God's word can be communicated through all of these. What type of literature do you consider Jonah to be? Why?" The Leader's Guide suggests that Jonah can be described as "a short story with a didactic purpose, a sermon, or a longer parable," but gives the leader permission to skip quickly over the whole question if this seems best. This is typical of the friendly, non-controversial tone of the entire program.

See: Friendship Bible Study Series, p. 215

1. Up-to-date historical critical scholarship incorporated?		**Yes**
2. Background information emphasized?		**No**
3. Application to personal and family life emphasized?		**Yes**
4. Application to the life and mission of the church included?		**Yes**
5. Application to broader social issues included?		**Yes**
6. Sexist language avoided?		**Yes**

7. Guidance for prayer at group meetings provided? **Yes**

8. Discussion questions provided? **Yes**

9. Practical directions for group leaders provided? **Yes**

10. Biblical background for group leaders provided? **Yes**

11. Biblical background for group members presumed? **No**

12. Participants required to prepare for each session? **Yes**

Old Testament

* THE PILGRIM GOD: A BIBLICAL JOURNEY.

Brother John of Taize. The Pastoral Press. 1985. 220 pp., 6 x 9. $13.95. 8 sessions.

These profound reflections trace the themes of pilgrim God and pilgrim people through the Hebrew scriptures. Excellent use is made of contemporary scholarship to find the significance of scripture for life today. Brother John, a member of an ecumenical monastic community, has read widely and integrated much scholarship into this contemplative review of the Hebrew scriptures. This book can serve as a fine review of the Hebrew scriptures as well as a profound study of the journey theme.

Each of the eight chapters gives suggested scripture readings and questions for reflection and discussion. The questions encourage reflection on personal experience and social issues. Very highly recommended for experienced, well educated groups willing to prepare seriously for each session and to share their personal journeys.

See: The Way of the Lord: A New Testament Pilgrimage. p. 117

1. Up-to-date historical critical scholarship incorporated?	**Yes**	
2. Background information emphasized?	**Yes**	
3. Application to personal and family life emphasized?	**Yes**	
4. Application to the life and mission of the church included?	**Yes**	
5. Application to broader social issues included?	**Yes**	
6. Sexist language avoided?	**Yes**	
7. Guidance for prayer at group meetings provided?	**No**	
8. Discussion questions provided?	**Yes**	
9. Practical directions for group leaders provided?	**No**	
10. Biblical background for group leaders provided?	**No**	
11. Biblical background for group members presumed?	**Yes**	
12. Participants required to prepare for each session?	**Yes**	

Old Testament

THE STORY OF THE OLD TESTAMENT COVENANT.

De Sales. Franciscan Communications, 1985. imprimatur. 4 videos, each containing two sessions, one hour each, 1 facilitator's guide, 1 participant's manual, $385. Additional participant's manuals, 116 pp., 8 ½ x 11. $6.50 each. 8 sessions.

This very rapid overview of the Old Testament contains a great deal of good information, probably more than most groups can absorb in eight sessions. The lectures are excellent, and might be used separately if one omitted the introductory and concluding sections with the hostess. Generally the material in the part of the lecture before the break is quite different from that covered after the break. A creative group leader might use one half of the lecture for a whole session, adding assigned scripture readings and questions.

As usual in this series, great care is taken to make the material relevant to the ordinary Catholic and to avoid shock as much as possible. For instance, Esther, Jonah, Ruth, and Job are treated without reference to their fictional form.

The last lecture consists mainly in the prayerful reading of several psalms with some pictures given in the background as an aid to meditation.

See: De Sales Program, p. 211

1.	Up-to-date historical critical scholarship incorporated?	**Yes**
2.	Background information emphasized?	**Yes**
3.	Application to personal and family life emphasized?	**Yes**
4.	Application to the life and mission of the church included?	**Yes**
5.	Application to broader social issues included?	**Yes**
6.	Sexist language avoided?	**Yes**
7.	Guidance for prayer at group meetings provided?	**Yes**
8.	Discussion questions provided?	**Yes**
9.	Practical directions for group leaders provided?	**Yes**
10.	Biblical background for group leaders provided?	**No**

11. Biblical background for group members presumed?   **No**

12. Participants required to prepare for each session?   **No**

FLIGHT TO FREEDOM: A FOUR-SESSION SMALL-GROUP BIBLE STUDY ON THE EXODUS.
Marcella Boyd. Small-Group Bible Study. Augsburg, 1976. 16 pp., 5 ½ x 8 ¼. $.90.

These discussion questions will aid groups wishing to read Exodus and find its implications for their lives without getting into scholarly background material. The bibliography lacks Catholic resources, but there is no reason why Catholics or members of other denominations could not benefit from this Lutheran program. This is an interesting, easy-to-use program and should be especially effective in an ecumenical group.

See: **Small Group Bible Study, p. 227.**

1.	Up-to-date historical critical scholarship incorporated?	**No**
2.	Background information emphasized?	**No**
3.	Application to personal and family life emphasized?	**Yes**
4.	Application to the life and mission of the church included?	**Yes**
5.	Application to broader social issues included?	**Yes**
6.	Sexist language avoided?	**No**
7.	Guidance for prayer at group meetings provided?	**Yes**
8.	Discussion questions provided?	**Yes**
9.	Practical directions for group leaders provided?	**No**
10.	Biblical background for group leaders provided?	**No**
11.	Biblical background for group members presumed?	**No**
12.	Participants required to prepare for each session?	**Yes**

ISRAEL BECOMES A PEOPLE.
Conrad L'Heureux, Lawrence Boadt, C.S.P., Robert M. Hamma. Paulist Bible Study Program. Paulist Press, 1990. Leader's Manual: 119 pp., 8 ½ x 11, $12.95. Workbook: 90 pp., 7 ¼ x 9 ¼, $3.95. Textbook: Reading the Old Testament by Lawrence Boadt, 569 pp., 6x9, $8.95. Video: 120 minutes, $79.95. 8 sessions.

This segment of the Paulist Bible Study Program covers methods of biblical criticism, biblical geography and archaeology, an overview of the Old Testament, the Pentateuch, Joshua, and Judges. Most of the problems in this otherwise excellent program come from the effort to cover so much material in eight sessions.

The prayer and faith sharing sections are very creatively and competently done. Several suggestions are usually given for songs, with indications of where they can be found. Simple rituals, excellent guided meditations, and a variety of selections from Catholic devotional tradition are utilized. The faith sharing exercises are also very well done, but may require more self disclosure more quickly than all participants are ready for. A highly skilled facilitator is needed for the faith sharing exercises.

Many participants will find the textbook chapter assigned each week heavy reading. The "Review of Contents" deals mainly with this material. This discussion is likely to bog down unless the leader or a resource person has a good background in Old Testament scholarship. With a good teacher in charge, the review will be extremely valuable.

At the beginning, the student is encouraged to give priority to reading the Bible itself rather than to the textbook, but few questions are given to assist in focusing on the biblical text assigned, so there is danger that it will not be fully appreciated. Emphasis on the academic material is strong. Difficult historical critical material is handled, sometimes with presentations of various scholarly positions. A beginning group would find all this difficult to digest so quickly.

The videos add a fine visual dimension to the experience, but not all are equally valuable. Those on biblical geography and archaeology cover so much material so rapidly that viewers are not likely to get more than a general impression. They would have more value if the relevant chapter from the textbook had been read before they were viewed, but these chapters are only recommended as optional follow-up reading.

The video on myth is excellent, effectively utilizing Joseph Campbell and examples from various cultures. The one on "Remembering the Exodus" includes appealing scenes of a contemporary Passover celebration and the Easter Vigil, and would make good viewing for anyone during Holy Week. "The Covenant and the Law," like other parts of this program, shows an interest in and sensitivity to Judaism. The final video on "The Importance of the Land of Israel" would be of interest to those concerned about contemporary Israel and especially Jerusalem as a center for three world religions.

Groups may not find the time allotted to the various activities adequate. This could be dealt with either by extending the meeting time to two and a half hours or by requiring participants to write the answers to the review questions in advance instead of doing it during the session as suggested. A group that wanted to do the program thoroughly, including the recommended reading, might choose to meet once a month for three or four hours.

This is a difficult program because of the amount of material dealt with in a short time. For a well educated group with a leader well trained in scripture and facilitation skills, it is excellent.

See: Paulist Bible Study Program, p. 221

1. Up-to-date historical critical scholarship incorporated?	Yes
2. Background information emphasized?	Yes
3. Application to personal and family life emphasized?	No
4. Application to the life and mission of the church included?	Yes
5. Application to broader social issues included?	Yes
6. Sexist language avoided?	Yes
7. Guidance for prayer at group meetings provided?	Yes
8. Discussion questions provided?	Yes
9. Practical directions for group leaders provided?	Yes
10. Biblical background for group leaders provided?	Yes
11. Biblical background for group members presumed?	No
12. Participants required to prepare for each session?	Yes

Old Testament

JOSEPH: FINDING GOD'S STRENGTH IN TIME OF TRIAL.

Gene A. Getz. Gospel Light Publications, 1983. Participant's Book: 151 pp., 8 ½ x 11. $6.95. Leader's Guide (1989): 168 pp., 5 x 8. $13.95. 13 sessions.

This program provides 13 sessions on the story of Joseph from Genesis, developed with the use of many passages from other parts of scripture. Joseph's story is analyzed with much psychological insight and used as a starting point for practical reflections on issues of family and, occasionally, business life. The aberrations of the family life of the patriarchs are faced and used as encouragement for problem families today. Only very rarely does the fundamentalist leaning of the author show. His sound psychological insights are much more conspicuous.

The participant's book consists of devotional readings for use between sessions. Occasionally parts of it are read aloud at the group session. Preparation by participants is recommended, but not essential. The leader would need both books, but participants would not have to have books at all.

The leader's guide contains excellent lesson plans for one hour sessions, along with biblical background and an abundance of very practical suggestions and attractive handouts which may be reproduced for group use. Leaders not in the Evangelical tradition may wish to supplement the biblical background with other material utilizing historical critical scholarship. But even a beginning teacher could conduct a lively and effective adult class by using the methods given. Participants' own life experiences are elicited in an opening exercise so that they can be used as an interpretive tool. The "Bible Exploration" occasionally includes brief presentations by the leader or a group member, but consists mostly in a variety of activities in which small groups (often two or three) work with specific Bible passages. The conclusion usually includes opportunity for a spontaneous prayer. The variety of teaching methods keeps everyone actively involved.

More intellectually inclined groups may feel the lack of scholarly material and resent the way the program tells them what the message of a passage is rather than leading them to read the scripture to find the message for themselves. But for groups that lack background and time for study, this may be an ideal program.

1. Up-to-date historical critical scholarship incorporated?   **No**

2. Background information emphasized?   **No**

3. Application to personal and family life emphasized?   **Yes**

4. Application to the life and mission of the church included?   **Yes**

---

5. Application to broader social issues included?   No

6. Sexist language avoided?   No

7. Guidance for prayer at group meetings provided?   Yes

8. Discussion questions provided?   Yes

9. Practical directions for group leaders provided?   Yes

10. Biblical background for group leaders provided?   Yes

11. Biblical background for group members presumed?   No

12. Participants required to prepare for each session?   No

JOSEPH: FROM PIT TO PINNACLE.
Charles R. Swindoll. Word, 1982. 44 pp., 5 ½ x 8 ½. $3.99. 12 sessions.

Joseph is presented as a model for behavior in family and business life. No attention is given to historical critical questions. References to the Rapture and to Jehovah mark this book as geared to an Evangelical readership, but it presents no serious theological problem for readers of other traditions. Recommended for beginning groups of limited educational background who wish to apply scripture to their lives immediately, without becoming involved in scholarly work.

See: Charles R. Swindoll Bible Study Guides , p. 229

1.	Up-to-date historical critical scholarship incorporated?	No
2.	Background information emphasized?	No
3.	Application to personal and family life emphasized?	Yes
4.	Application to the life and mission of the church included?	No
5.	Application to broader social issues included?	No
6.	Sexist language avoided?	No
7.	Guidance for prayer at group meetings provided?	No
8.	Discussion questions provided?	No
9.	Practical directions for group leaders provided?	No
10.	Biblical background for group leaders provided?	No
11.	Biblical background for group members presumed?	No
12.	Participants required to prepare for each session?	Yes

HAND ME ANOTHER BRICK: A STUDY OF NEHEMIAH.
Charles R. Swindoll. Word, 1990. 125 pp., 5 ½ x 8 ½. $4.99. 16 sessions.

This booklet offers 16 lessons on Nehemiah, showing him as a model of leadership. Much practical advice about leadership and encouragement of Christians to accept leadership positions is included. However, the value of unknown collaborators is also pointed out. Nehemiah is compared to Churchill. Both are seen as ideal leaders, with little mention of their human weaknesses. This book does not raise any theological problems which should discourage Christians of any tradition from using it. Recommended for beginning groups wanting simple applications of biblical texts without becoming involved in scholarship.

See: Charles R. Swindoll Bible Study Guides , p. 229

1.	Up-to-date historical critical scholarship incorporated?	**No**
2.	Background information emphasized?	**Yes**
3.	Application to personal and family life emphasized?	**Yes**
4.	Application to the life and mission of the church included?	**Yes**
5.	Application to broader social issues included?	**No**
6.	Sexist language avoided?	**No**
7.	Guidance for prayer at group meetings provided?	**No**
8.	Discussion questions provided?	**No**
9.	Practical directions for group leaders provided?	**No**
10.	Biblical background for group leaders provided?	**No**
11.	Biblical background for group members presumed?	**No**
12.	Participants required to prepare for each session?	**Yes**

Old Testament

Historical Writings

THE LIFE OF DAVID.

Larry Fourman. Covenant Bible Studies. Brethren Press, 1990. 40 pp., 5½ x 8½. $2.95. 10 sessions.

This is a study of selected chapters from 1 and 2 Samuel and 1 Kings dealing with David's relationships with Samuel, Saul, Jonathan, God, Mephibosheth, Bathsheba, Nathan, the infant son who died, and Solomon. The commentary mainly retells the stories. David is called author of the Psalms, an opinion with which few contemporary scholars would agree. However, the lack of use of historical critical scholarship does not generally create problems in this story-telling approach.

There is a strong emphasis on church life, and it is evident that the booklet is intended for members of the Church of the Brethren. However, there is no serious reason why it cannot be adapted by others.

Participants are expected for each session to read one or two chapters of scripture and the three and a half page commentary, and to answer questions which challenge them both to analyze and to apply the text.

Discussion suggestions are also provided. Some are creative activities, such as writing a parable to challenge some contemporary evil as Nathan's parable challenged David. Others call for dramatic reading of the text. Some call for sharing of personal and family experiences on a deep level with which not everyone will be comfortable.

See: Covenant Bible Studies, p. 209

1. Up-to-date historical critical scholarship incorporated? No

2. Background information emphasized? No

3. Application to personal and family life emphasized? Yes

4. Application to the life and mission of the church included? Yes

5. Application to broader social issues included? Yes

6. Sexist language avoided? Yes

7. Guidance for prayer at group meetings provided? No

8. Discussion questions provided? Yes

9. Practical directions for group leaders provided?   **No**

10. Biblical background for group leaders provided?   **No**

11. Biblical background for group members presumed?   **No**

12. Participants required to prepare for each session?   **Yes**

Old Testament

AMOS AND HOSEA.

Hemchand Gossai. Men's Bible Study Series. Augsburg, 1989. Study Book: 48 pp., 4 ½ x 9 ½. $2.85. Leader Guide: 32 pp., 4 ½ x 9 ½. $3.10. 10 sessions.

The first five sessions each deal with a brief passage from the Book of Amos. Many questions about contemporary issues are raised: international relations, war, business ethics, ecology, and closing stores on Sunday. The questions are open ended and likely to stir up lively discussion. The leader is told to expect differing opinions, not to try to force certain ideas. What does come through is a clear call to integrate worship, family, work, social and political life.

The second five sessions deal with passages from Hosea, emphasizing more specifically religious issues. Participants are often asked to compare the passage being studied with other passages in scripture.

See: Men's Bible Study Series, p. 219

1.	Up-to-date historical critical scholarship incorporated?	**Yes**
2.	Background information emphasized?	**No**
3.	Application to personal and family life emphasized?	**Yes**
4.	Application to the life and mission of the church included?	**Yes**
5.	Application to broader social issues included?	**Yes**
6.	Sexist language avoided?	**Yes**
7.	Guidance for prayer at group meetings provided?	**Yes**
8.	Discussion questions provided?	**Yes**
9.	Practical directions for group leaders provided?	**Yes**
10.	Biblical background for group leaders provided?	**Yes**
11.	Biblical background for group members presumed?	**No**
12.	Participants required to prepare for each session?	**No**

THE BOOK OF JONAH: A STUDY GUIDE.

Daniele D. Flannery and John R. Schmitz. Hi-Time, 1985. imprimatur. 24 pp., 8 ½ x 11. $4.25 for a single copy; $2.95 each if 5 or more copies are ordered. 4 sessions.

These four lessons provide an easy and pleasant starting point for scripture study, especially for a group which does not want to prepare between sessions. One of the four chapters of the Book of Jonah is read aloud at each session. Then each participant reads it again silently, answering in a workbook simple questions about the text. Then a page or so of "Points for Understanding" provide some background material. Finally, several good questions are provided for personal reflection and sharing about the implications of the chapter for Christians and for Christian communities today. Participants are challenged to find these implications for themselves; the approach is not preachy. At the end of the book two pages are devoted to explaining that Jonah is a parable and quoting the Constitution on Divine Revelation from the Second Vatican Council about the need to recognize literary forms. Especially recommended for beginning groups.

1.	Up-to-date historical critical scholarship incorporated?	**Yes**
2.	Background information emphasized?	**Yes**
3.	Application to personal and family life emphasized?	**Yes**
4.	Application to the life and mission of the church included?	**Yes**
5.	Application to broader social issues included?	**Yes**
6.	Sexist language avoided?	**Yes**
7.	Guidance for prayer at group meetings provided?	**No**
8.	Discussion questions provided?	**Yes**
9.	Practical directions for group leaders provided?	**Yes**
10.	Biblical background for group leaders provided?	**No**
11.	Biblical background for group members presumed?	**No**
12.	Participants required to prepare for each session?	**No**

* ISAIAH.

Terence Y. Mullins. Friendship Bible Study Series. Augsburg, 1988. Study Book: 48 pp., 5 ½ x 8 ½. $2.85. Leader Guide: 32 pp., 5 ½ x 8 ½. $3.10. 8 sessions.

This remarkable study manages to treat a difficult prophet with respect for scholarly interpretations and yet make him not only intelligible but also highly relevant to contemporary Christians.

First, Second, and Third Isaiah are set in their historical backgrounds and are said to deal respectively with sin, forgiveness, and renewal. Fine insights about the relationship between Judah and the super powers of the eighth century before Christ lead into probing questions about Christian responsibility in the modern world. The brief prayer responses are particularly fine.

The author shows good judgement in including the historical background necessary for understanding Isaiah without overloading the participants for whom this series is intended.

See: **Friendship Bible Study Series, p. 215**

1. Up-to-date historical critical scholarship incorporated?	**Yes**
2. Background information emphasized?	**No**
3. Application to personal and family life emphasized?	**Yes**
4. Application to the life and mission of the church included?	**Yes**
5. Application to broader social issues included?	**Yes**
6. Sexist language avoided?	**Yes**
7. Guidance for prayer at group meetings provided?	**Yes**
8. Discussion questions provided?	**Yes**
9. Practical directions for group leaders provided?	**Yes**
10. Biblical background for group leaders provided?	**Yes**
11. Biblical background for group members presumed?	**No**
12. Participants required to prepare for each session?	**Yes**

Old Testament

PRE-EXILIC PROPHETS.
Mary Mauren. Scripture Share and Prayer. 1985. Looseleaf binder containing 12 audiotapes, 60 minutes each, and 50 pp., 8 ½ x 11 of study guides which may be reproduced. $75. 12 to 16 sessions.

This program deals primarily with Amos, Hosea, Isaiah of Jerusalem, Micah, and Jeremiah. Because of the emphasis on historical background, a considerable amount of material from the Books of Kings is also included. Participants should at least have completed the Scripture Foundations program in this series. Those with more scripture background will enjoy it more.

There are 12 sessions covering the basic material, plus four optional sessions spaced throughout to integrate and review.

Mary Mauren uses her teaching skills to bring the prophets and their times to life, but this program also requires much time and commitment from participants.

See: Scripture Share and Prayer, p.225

1.	Up-to-date historical critical scholarship incorporated?	**Yes**
2.	Background information emphasized?	**Yes**
3.	Application to personal and family life emphasized?	**Yes**
4.	Application to the life and mission of the church included?	**Yes**
5.	Application to broader social issues included?	**Yes**
6.	Sexist language avoided?	**Yes**
7.	Guidance for prayer at group meetings provided?	**No**
8.	Discussion questions provided?	**Yes**
9.	Practical directions for group leaders provided?	**No**
10.	Biblical background for group leaders provided?	**No**
11.	Biblical background for group members presumed?	**Yes**
12.	Participants required to prepare for each session?	**Yes**

Old Testament

PROVERBS.

Mary Y. Nilsen. Friendship Bible Study Series. Augsburg, 1987. Study Book: 48 pp., 5 ½ x 8 ½. $2.85. Leader Guide: 32 pp., 5 ½ x 8 ½. $3.10. 8 sessions.

This program is recommended for ecumenical groups because Proverbs deals with matters of everyday life which draw people together and does not touch on the doctrinal matters that divide churches. Proverbs is not read through consecutively, but selected proverbs are used to discuss such topics as images of God, life long learning, temptation, the power of words, money, personal relationships, family life, and friendship. Plenty of good common sense psychology and opportunity for personal sharing are included. This is not a simplistic looking to the Bible for instructions on modern life. Passages from elsewhere in the Bible are brought in as appropriate to balance Proverbs. Each session closes with the Serenity Prayer. Groups using these booklets can expect a fruitful experience of Christian sharing.

See: **Friendship Bible Study Series, p. 215**

1.	Up-to-date historical critical scholarship incorporated?	**Yes**
2.	Background information emphasized?	**No**
3.	Application to personal and family life emphasized?	**Yes**
4.	Application to the life and mission of the church included?	**Yes**
5.	Application to broader social issues included?	**Yes**
6.	Sexist language avoided?	**Yes**
7.	Guidance for prayer at group meetings provided?	**No**
8.	Discussion questions provided?	**Yes**
9.	Practical directions for group leaders provided?	**Yes**
10.	Biblical background for group leaders provided?	**Yes**
11.	Biblical background for group members presumed?	**No**
12.	Participants required to prepare for each session?	**Yes**

* PSALMS.

John David Bowman. Covenant Bible Studies. Brethren Press, 1989. 40 pp., 8 ½ x 5 ½. $2.95. 10 sessions.

Through this study of psalms, participants should come to appreciate the emotions as an appropriate arena for our relationship with God. The biblical psalms are used to uncover our emotions: praise, anguish, despair, loneliness, anger, joy, guilt, awe, and fear. The author points out that many psalms provide outlets for feelings that would become destructive if not expressed and challenges the assumption that people of faith should be exempt from strong negative feelings.

Each session contains three-and-a-half pages of excellent commentary on the psalms being studied. The author draws on wide reading, including insights from varied Christian, Jewish and secular sources. Reference is also made to related parts of scripture which can sometimes be used to balance dangerously literal interpretations of certain verses.

Cultural and religious background from the Ancient Near East is also brought to bear on the psalms studied. The reader sees how much in the psalms is adapted from Canaanite religion, in spite of the strong biblical rejection of the essentials of that religion. This leads to a challenge to consider whether there are contemporary secular forms which ought to be adapted into Christian worship.

This program does not pause for the usual introductory material on psalms but goes directly into the study of specific psalms: 4, 90, 146, 147, 150, 13, 130, 123, 142, 58, 96, 133, 38, 51, 8, 104, 91, 32, and 139.

In preparation for each session, participants are to read from one to three psalms, read the commentary, and answer a few questions (which generally relate the psalm to personal, national, or international experience or develop its key ideas). There is little detailed analysis of the text. Some questions call for journal reflection, prayer, or concrete action in applying the psalm.

The additional questions provided for discussion are insightful and should lead to lively and fruitful discussion covering a range of issues dealing not only with personal emotions, but also with sensitivity to minorities, ecology, and other peace and justice issues. Several times the group is called to "covenant with each other" to a specific action for the week.

This is an exceptionally high quality program both for its use of biblical scholarship and its sensitivity to contemporary issues.

See: Covenant Bible Studies, p. 209

1.	Up-to-date historical critical scholarship incorporated?	**Yes**
2.	Background information emphasized?	**No**
3.	Application to personal and family life emphasized?	**Yes**
4.	Application to the life and mission of the church included?	**Yes**
5.	Application to broader social issues included?	**Yes**
6.	Sexist language avoided?	**Yes**
7.	Guidance for prayer at group meetings provided?	**No**
8.	Discussion questions provided?	**Yes**
9.	Practical directions for group leaders provided?	**No**
10.	Biblical background for group leaders provided?	**No**
11.	Biblical background for group members presumed?	**No**
12.	Participants required to prepare for each session?	**Yes**

Old Testament

PSALMS.

Frederick J. Gaiser. Men's Bible Study Series. Augsburg, 1988. Study Book: 48 pp., 4 ½ x 9 ½. $2.85. Leader Guide: 32 pp., 4 ½ x 9 ½. $3.10. 10 sessions.

These sessions deal with what the psalms teach us about ourselves, God and our neighbor. The principal psalms treated are 8, 51, 16, 41, 133, 67, 148, 95, 66, and 23. Participants are sent to many related passages in the psalms and elsewhere in scripture. Connections are also made with congregational worship.

The booklet does not include the general material usually given in an introduction to the psalms.

See: **Men's Bible Study Series, p. 219**

1.	Up-to-date historical critical scholarship incorporated?	**Yes**
2.	Background information emphasized?	**No**
3.	Application to personal and family life emphasized?	**Yes**
4.	Application to the life and mission of the church included?	**Yes**
5.	Application to broader social issues included?	**Yes**
6.	Sexist language avoided?	**Yes**
7.	Guidance for prayer at group meetings provided?	**Yes**
8.	Discussion questions provided?	**Yes**
9.	Practical directions for group leaders provided?	**Yes**
10.	Biblical background for group leaders provided?	**Yes**
11.	Biblical background for group members presumed?	**No**
12.	Participants required to prepare for each session?	**No**

Reviews of Individual Programs

Section III:
New Testament

BEGINNERS' GUIDE TO BIBLE SHARING: VOLUME I.

John Burke, O.P. Brown, 1984. imprimatur. 186 pp., 8 ¼ x 10 ¾. $10.95. 60 sessions.

This program aims to introduce Catholics to the Bible in a way that will touch their hearts and lives and provide them with the skills which will enable them to continue Bible study on their own.

A fairly short scripture passage is studied each session (less than a chapter in the first thirty sessions; up to two chapters in the study of Acts). Each session begins with an opening prayer created by the leader to highlight the themes of the passage and time to resolve any questions left over from the previous session. Then the passage for the day is read aloud and discussed, using the abundant discussion questions provided. Most of the time is spent on discussion. The session ends with spontaneous prayer.

Participants must be willing to share their religious experience and also to prepare for each session, using footnotes in their Bibles and reference books. There is little input in this book itself; participants are expected to learn to find information for themselves and share it in the group. Occasionally volunteers are asked to do special research projects and report to the group.

The strength of the program is its questions, which are brief and easily understood. Some challenge understanding of the text, others application. Very occasionally, a charismatic background is suggested by the questions (e.g. "Have you accepted Jesus Christ as Lord and Savior?" "How do you as a Christian bear witness to Jesus in the power of the Spirit?"). Questions challenge participants to evangelization more frequently than to social justice concerns.

Father Burke recommends that leadership rotate within the group. This might be difficult with a beginning group. The leader is responsible for leading in spontaneous prayer and for briefly introducing the scripture to be studied, in addition to frequently summarizing and facilitating the discussion.

There is an emphasis on Catholic teaching throughout. A bibliography is provided but should be expanded with books published since 1984.

The first 30 sessions deal with themes (e.g. "God Chose Us," "The Power of Sin," "The Fruits of the Spirit," "The Church of Jesus," "The Law of Love"). Texts are selected from throughout the New Testament and there is little continuity from session to session, so sessions could well be used independently of each other by a group not wanting to do the entire 30. This material is elementary, and some groups may prefer to omit it.

The second 30 sessions deal with the Acts of the Apostles but also include som
relevant passages from Paul. Since the whole of Acts is read, it will be more satisfyir
than the first 30 sessions for groups which wish to read passages in context or 1
experience some continuity in their study.

See: **Beginners' Guide to Bible Sharing, Volume II, p. 107**

1.	Up-to-date historical critical scholarship incorporated?	**Yes**
2.	Background information emphasized?	**No**
3.	Application to personal and family life emphasized?	**Yes**
4.	Application to the life and mission of the church included?	**Yes**
5.	Application to broader social issues included?	**Yes**
6.	Sexist language avoided?	**Yes**
7.	Guidance for prayer at group meetings provided?	**No**
8.	Discussion questions provided?	**Yes**
9.	Practical directions for group leaders provided?	**Yes**
10.	Biblical background for group leaders provided?	**No**
11.	Biblical background for group members presumed?	**No**
12.	Participants required to prepare for each session?	**Yes**

BEGINNERS' GUIDE TO BIBLE SHARING: VOLUME II.

John Burke, O.P. Brown, 1984. imprimatur. 228 pp., 8 ¼ x 10 ¾. $11.95. 60 sessions.

This volume follows the same format as Volume I but is geared to a more advanced group. Though prayer is encouraged during the sessions, the form of prayer is left to the leader. There are fewer elementary and more challenging questions, including some optional questions for still more advanced groups. Some questions are intended to evoke soul-searching insight into one's inner self.

All of Luke is covered in order in the first 30 sessions, all of Romans in the second. Considerably more introductory and explanatory material is provided for Romans, including a condensed paraphrase of the famous letter on the subject by C.H. Dodd. Father Burke is aware of the complexities of this letter and the Reformation controversies based on it. However, he continues to rely principally on research done in other books to provide needed background. Whether or not participants come out of this program with a reasonably accurate understanding of the texts will depend to a considerable extent on the quality of outside reference books and the quality of reports given from them by group members.

This is a good program for groups motivated to wrestle with the difficulties of Romans, but, despite the title, it is <u>not</u> a book for beginners.

See: Beginners' Guide to Bible Sharing, Volume II, p. 105

1. Up-to-date historical critical scholarship incorporated? **Yes**

2. Background information emphasized? **No**

3. Application to personal and family life emphasized? **Yes**

4. Application to the life and mission of the church included? **Yes**

5. Application to broader social issues included? **Yes**

6. Sexist language avoided? **Yes**

7. Guidance for prayer at group meetings provided? **No**

8. Discussion questions provided? **Yes**

9. Practical directions for group leaders provided? **Yes**

10. Biblical background for group leaders provided?   **No**

11. Biblical background for group members presumed?   **No**

12. Participants required to prepare for each session?   **Yes**

New Testament

A GUIDE TO READING THE NEW TESTAMENT: PART ONE--THE MYSTERY OF JESUS.

ACTA Publications, 1986 (revised edition). imprimatur. 96 pp., 5 ¼ x 8. $2.50.
8 sessions.

This is a continuation of *A Guide to Reading the Old Testament*, in the same attractive format. It is presumed that participants have been through the Old Testament part of the program. The topics for discussion effectively challenge participants to apply the scripture to their lives.

The biblical books dealt with are Acts, Mark, 1 Peter, Matthew, 1 John, and John's Gospel.

Unfortunately, there is a great deal of factual material, and much of it, while based on traditional ideas, is not in harmony with contemporary scientific biblical scholarship. Participants are told that Matthew and John were eyewitnesses of the life of Jesus, that the Apostle John lived in Ephesus and wrote the Gospel and 1 John, etc. A participant who continued in another Catholic or mainline program would have a great deal to unlearn. Available in Spanish.

See: A Guide to Reading the New Testament: Part Two, p. 111
A Guide to Reading the Old Testament: Part One, p. 67

1. Up-to-date historical critical scholarship incorporated?   **No**

2. Background information emphasized?   **Yes**

3. Application to personal and family life emphasized?   **Yes**

4. Application to the life and mission of the church included?   **Yes**

5. Application to broader social issues included?   **Yes**

6. Sexist language avoided?   **No**

7. Guidance for prayer at group meetings provided?   **No**

8. Discussion questions provided?   **Yes**

9. Practical directions for group leaders provided?   **No**

10. Biblical background for group leaders provided?   **No**

11. Biblical background for group members presumed?   **No**

12. Participants required to prepare for each session?   **Yes**

GUIDE TO READING THE NEW TESTAMENT:
ART TWO--THE WHOLE CHRIST.

CTA Publications, 1985 (revised edition). imprimatur. 94 pp., 5 ¼ x 8. $2.50.
sessions.

his program continues the same format as Part One, reviewed on page 109, with the
ame problems. Participants are told that 2 Timothy is by Paul, the woman in the
ook of Revelation is the Virgin Mary, Luke was a physician and companion of Paul
vhose gospel can be considered "the Gospel of Paul," etc. Biblical books dealt with
re Acts, Luke, Galatians, 1 Corinthians, Philemon, Philippians, 2 Timothy, and
.evelation. Available in Spanish.

ee: **A Guide to Reading the New Testament: Part One, p. 109**
     A Guide to Reading the Old Testament: Part One, p. 67

1. Up-to-date historical critical scholarship incorporated?	**No**
2. Background information emphasized?	**Yes**
3. Application to personal and family life emphasized?	**Yes**
4. Application to the life and mission of the church included?	**Yes**
5. Application to broader social issues included?	**Yes**
6. Sexist language avoided?	**No**
7. Guidance for prayer at group meetings provided?	**No**
8. Discussion questions provided?	**Yes**
9. Practical directions for group leaders provided?	**No**
10. Biblical background for group leaders provided?	**No**
11. Biblical background for group members presumed?	**No**
12. Participants required to prepare for each session?	**Yes**

INTRODUCTION TO NEW TESTAMENT STUDIES.

William A. Anderson. Benziger New Testament Study Series. Benziger, 1988. Imprimatur. 59 pp., 5 ¼ x 8. $4.68. 4 sessions.

This is an introduction to a 12 volume study of the New Testament. This introduction contains a chapter summarizing the history of Israel and the religious background of Jesus' time, one on the development of the New Testament canon, one on how the gospels developed, and a brief one on "The Real Jesus" which aims at calming people distressed to learn that the gospels are not biographies in the modern sense.

This booklet presents an enormous amount of material in digest style. Information based on contemporary scholarship, but space does not permit clarification of which points are still controversial among scholars. The reading is lightened slightly by occasional contemporary examples.

Each of the four chapters is followed by review questions and reflection questions. A group wishing to use this book for four sessions could use these questions. Most groups will find this book more valuable as background reading for members to do on their own before or while using one of the other books in the series.

See: Benziger New Testament Study Series, p. 205

1.	Up-to-date historical critical scholarship incorporated?	**Yes**
2.	Background information emphasized?	**Yes**
3.	Application to personal and family life emphasized?	**No**
4.	Application to the life and mission of the church included?	**No**
5.	Application to broader social issues included?	**No**
6.	Sexist language avoided?	**Yes**
7.	Guidance for prayer at group meetings provided?	**No**
8.	Discussion questions provided?	**Yes**
9.	Practical directions for group leaders provided?	**No**
10.	Biblical background for group leaders provided?	**No**

11. Biblical background for group members presumed?   **No**

12. Participants required to prepare for each session?   **Yes**

JOHN, GALATIANS: EXPOSING RELIGIOUS COUNTERFEITS.
Serendipity Group Bible Study. Serendipity, 1988. 64 pp., 6 ½ x 9. $4.95. 12 to 21 sessions.

This program has the same format, strengths, and weaknesses as *Philippians, Ephesians* in the same series.

Though the content of the commentary is generally acceptable, it differs from the majority of Catholic and mainline scholars in stating that 1 John was written by the Apostle John and in preferring the South Galatian to the North Galatian theory about the destination of the Letter to the Galatians. (Related to this is an earlier dating for Galatians than most scholars would support.)

See: Philippians, Ephesians, p. 185

1. Up-to-date historical critical scholarship incorporated?	**No**
2. Background information emphasized?	**No**
3. Application to personal and family life emphasized?	**Yes**
4. Application to the life and mission of the church included?	**Yes**
5. Application to broader social issues included?	**Yes**
6. Sexist language avoided?	**Yes**
7. Guidance for prayer at group meetings provided?	**No**
8. Discussion questions provided?	**Yes**
9. Practical directions for group leaders provided?	**No**
10. Biblical background for group leaders provided?	**No**
11. Biblical background for group members presumed?	**No**
12. Participants required to prepare for each session?	**No**

THE WAY OF THE LORD: A NEW TESTAMENT PILGRIMAGE.
Brother John of Taize. Pastoral Press, 1990. 198 pp., 6 x 9. $13.95. 8 sessions.

This is a continuation of the author's *Pilgrim God* and is best used by groups which have discussed that book or at least have a good Old Testament background. Brother John sees the life of Christ as a recapitulation of the Old Testament, best understood in the light of its Jewish background. It is assumed that the reader knows that background.

Brother John's aim is to bridge the gap between scientific exegesis and theology/spirituality. In this he is highly successful. He is nourished by both contemporary critical studies and the older Christian tradition and goes beyond both to produce a synthesis full of insight for the spiritual journey of the Christian today.

The theme of "journey" is traced through the entire New Testament. We are shown that "The life of Jesus is a life on the road" and that Christianity is "a being-on-the-road with the guidance of the Holy Spirit." In a profound way, the reader is invited to participate in the journey. "When we meditate on the scriptures we are invited to take our place in a great epic, a drama that began the day an unknown God encountered Abraham on his journey..."

Almost two thirds of the book reflects on the gospels. This part, and those on Acts and Hebrews are particularly insightful.

Each chapter ends with four to six questions for reflection and discussion. Like the text itself, these are theological questions which often move into the depths of the scripture. They are not simple factual or application questions such as most programs provide. Theologically advanced groups will welcome their challenge.

Footnotes at the end of each chapter show the roots of Brother John's thinking in contemporary scholarship, especially French scholarship. They also show his broad ecumenical study, including the Orthodox tradition. These notes can easily be omitted. However, to properly understand each chapter it is necessary to look up the scripture references given.

This book is primarily geared to private reading, but could provide excellent material for discussion by a well educated group.

See: The Pilgrim God, p. 73

1. Up-to-date historical critical scholarship incorporated?   **Yes**

2. Background information emphasized?   **Yes**

3. Application to personal and family life emphasized?   **Yes**

4. Application to the life and mission of the church included?   **Yes**

5. Application to broader social issues included?   **Yes**

6. Sexist language avoided?   **Yes**

7. Guidance for prayer at group meetings provided?   **No**

8. Discussion questions provided?   **Yes**

9. Practical directions for group leaders provided?   **No**

10. Biblical background for group leaders provided?   **No**

11. Biblical background for group members presumed?   **Yes**

12. Participants required to prepare for each session?   **Yes**

BLESSED BY JESUS.

Bless Bible Studies for residents of health care centers and nursing homes. Augsburg, 1987. Participant book: 24 pp., 8 ¼ x 11. $2.70. Leader Guide: 48 pp., 8 ¼ x 11. $6.40. 12 sessions.

Gospel stories lead into discussion of these themes: Trust and faith, Friendship, child-like faith, Criticism, Healing, God hears, Forgiveness, Shared faith, Anger, being cared for, Preparing for death, Doubt and faith. Application of popular gospel stories to the life situation of nursing home residents brings rich insights. For example, the difficulty of the disciples in allowing Jesus to wash their feet is compared to the difficulty residents often experience in allowing others to care for their physical needs. On the cross, Jesus' concern to provide care for his widowed mother after his death is likened the family concerns of many elderly people. An excellent program.

See: Bless Bible Studies, p. 207

1. Up-to-date historical critical scholarship incorporated?	**No**
2. Background information emphasized?	**No**
3. Application to personal and family life emphasized?	**Yes**
4. Application to the life and mission of the church included?	**Yes**
5. Application to broader social issues included?	**No**
6. Sexist language avoided?	**Yes**
7. Guidance for prayer at group meetings provided?	**Yes**
8. Discussion questions provided?	**Yes**
9. Practical directions for group leaders provided?	**Yes**
10. Biblical background for group leaders provided?	**No**
11. Biblical background for group members presumed?	**No**
12. Participants required to prepare for each session?	**No**

DISCOVERING THE GOSPELS: FOUR ACCOUNTS OF THE GOOD NEWS.

Margaret Nutting Ralph. Discovering the Living Word Series. Paulist, 1990. 283 pp., 6 x 9. $11.95

This is an introduction to the gospels in a very unusual format. The student is instructed to read each gospel through carefully, without using introduction or footnotes, jotting down any questions that come to mind. The book consists of 72 questions which the author has found to be the most frequently asked, with a mini-lecture of about three pages in response to each. The lectures do not always give direct answers to the questions, but they are so constructed that eventually most of the material ordinarily covered in an introduction to the gospels is included. The method has the liveliness of a question and answer session, and also its problem: not everyone is interested in the answers to other people's questions. For the sake of participants whose questions are not included in the book, it would be important to have a resource person in the group who could help to deal with other questions.

Some questions answered are: "Wasn't it wrong for James and John to leave their father Zebedee in the boat?" "Why did Jesus teach in parables?" "Why did that poor guy get thrown out of the wedding feast? After all, it wasn't his fault he wasn't dressed properly." "Why didn't Jesus go to Lazarus immediately instead of waiting? Then he would have saved Martha and Mary all that grief." "I agree with the vineyard workers who complain that they weren't paid more than those who worked a shorter time. What is Jesus teaching in this parable?" The effect of a book which consists entirely in the answers to such questions is a bit patchwork. Some learners will miss a more organized presentation of the material; others will find the approach refreshing.

After the response to each question, review questions are given. These are particularly valuable if the book is used as an introduction to the New Testament, because much of the basic information inserted into the answers may be overlooked by readers focusing too narrowly on the questions. Discussion questions are also given, dealing with personal experience and opinions, more or less connected with the content of the segment. Some of the questions ask for opinions about matters not explained in the text, about which many participants will not have enough information to form an intelligent answer. This is more likely to hinder discussion in an adult group than in a teenage group.

The author indicates that the book is suitable for juniors in high school and anyone older. Discussion questions are occasionally geared to youth, but the material is easily adaptable to adults.

For lunch hour groups, the segments might be covered one at a time. For othe groups two or more segments might be covered in each session. If several segment are covered, the leader might have to select certain questions to be discusse Because the segments are so short they might be read during the session rather tha in preparation. However, the advance reading of the entire gospel by eac participant is essential to the program.

The content combines traditional interpretations with more current scholarly one: At times information is given without any indication that many scholars toda would disagree; at other times the variety of views is acknowledged. In the treatme of John's gospel, there is a strong emphasis on allegorical interpretation.

The many biblical quotations are from the old Revised Standard Version, whic introduces a fair number of generic masculine pronouns.

The book includes a very helpful glossary and an index of biblical references.

A group using another program to study the gospels might want a copy of this boo on hand for reference. Some of the questions answered here are likely to arise in an group.

1.	Up-to-date historical critical scholarship incorporated?	**Yes**
2.	Background information emphasized?	**Yes**
3.	Application to personal and family life emphasized?	**Yes**
4.	Application to the life and mission of the church included?	**Yes**
5.	Application to broader social issues included?	**Yes**
6.	Sexist language avoided?	**Yes**
7.	Guidance for prayer at group meetings provided?	**No**
8.	Discussion questions provided?	**Yes**
9.	Practical directions for group leaders provided?	**No**
10.	Biblical background for group leaders provided?	**No**
11.	Biblical background for group members presumed?	**No**
12.	Participants required to prepare for each session?	**Yes**

HOW TO READ AND PRAY THE GOSPELS.

Marilyn Norquist Gustin. Liguori, 1978. imprimatur. 64 pp., 5 x 7 ½. $2.50. 10 or 20 sessions.

This booklet aims to lead the beginner into the gospels. The approach is light and appealing. The reader is advised, "Read with a light heart. Expect to have fun--fun in discovery, delight in learning, pleasure in prayer."

The author has mastered the scholarly material well enough to be able to provide just enough solid background to enhance the beginner's exploration of the gospels. In between sessions participants are expected to read an entire gospel, noting well-selected points.

Discussion questions are well planned to provide springboards for discussion.

A variety of simple suggestions are included for praying with the gospels. There is much use of imagination in these prayer exercises and a loving, personal sense of Jesus. One who utilizes these exercises can expect to grow in prayer.

This program is unusual in that it can be adapted to family use. Special discussion questions and prayer suggestions are provided for families.

1.	Up-to-date historical critical scholarship incorporated?	**Yes**
2.	Background information emphasized?	**Yes**
3.	Application to personal and family life emphasized?	**Yes**
4.	Application to the life and mission of the church included?	**No**
5.	Application to broader social issues included?	**Yes**
6.	Sexist language avoided?	**No**
7.	Guidance for prayer at group meetings provided?	**No**
8.	Discussion questions provided?	**Yes**
9.	Practical directions for group leaders provided?	**Yes**
10.	Biblical background for group leaders provided?	**No**

11. Biblical background for group members presumed?　　　**No**

12. Participants required to prepare for each session?　　　**Yes**

New Testament

___

INVOLVING ADULTS IN THE BIBLE.
Brethren House, 1983. 58 pp., 8 ½ x 11. $8.00.

This is an outstanding program for teaching participants to meditate on gospel stories. It is based on the belief that "The Holy Spirit, having inspired the scriptures, can each day help people see their own reflections mirrored in passages they select." Participants are taught to personalize the words of scripture by using intuition and imagination.

Only the leader needs a copy of the book. Forms which participants will need may be reproduced from the book. A sensitive leader, comfortable in leading people in prayer, is needed. No biblical expertise is required. Clear, excellent directions are provided for the leader.

For each biblical story, five steps are taken: 1. Preparation (centering), 2. Pondering (careful reading), 3. Picture (a visualization led by the leader), 4. Prayer (a written dialogue with a character in the story) and 5. Promise (an application to life).

Excellent grids are provided to help with the pondering. For example, in encounter stories participants are asked to fill in the following: people encountered, the encounter, the results, my questions. Emphasis is on allowing one's own questions to surface, whether they are about the story itself or about its application to one's life. After everyone has worked silently filling this in, results are compared in groups of two or three. (A more in depth sharing takes place after the journal time.)

Eight visualizations are provided for the leader to read aloud while participants enter into the scene imaginatively. Instructions are also given for composing one's own visualizations. (For leaders who prefer ready made visualizations, more are available in *Visualizing Scripture*.)

The material here could be arranged for any number of sessions.

There is also a section teaching the regular use of a spiritual journal.

See: Visualizing Scripture, p. 143

1. Up-to-date historical critical scholarship incorporated?   **No**

2. Background information emphasized?   **No**

3. Application to personal and family life emphasized?   **Yes**

___

4. Application to the life and mission of the church included?   **Yes**

5. Application to broader social issues included?   **Yes**

6. Sexist language avoided?   **Yes**

7. Guidance for prayer at group meetings provided?   **Yes**

8. Discussion questions provided?   **Yes**

9. Practical directions for group leaders provided?   **Yes**

10. Biblical background for group leaders provided?   **No**

11. Biblical background for group members presumed?   **No**

12. Participants required to prepare for each session?   **No**

New Testament

* JESUS AND THE GOSPELS.

Paulist Bible Study Program. Paulist Press, 1990. Leader's Manual: 127 pp., 8 ½ x 11, $12.95. Workbook: 90 pp, 7 ¼ x 9 ¼, $3.95. Textbook: Reading the New Testament by Pheme Perkins, 350 pp., 6 x 9. $7.95. Video: 120 minutes, $79.95. 8 sessions.

This segment of the Paulist Bible Study Program contains an overview of the New Testament, historical background for the life of Jesus, the synoptic gospels, and a chapter each on the Resurrection and on Christology (including the early councils).

The prayer and faith sharing sections are well planned and do not require more than the average parish group will be comfortable with. There are not many options for songs, and sources for songs are not indicated.

Each week a chapter from the college level textbook is assigned. It is presumed that participants have read this, and both the "Review of Content" section and the "Learning Activity" consist of group activities digging into the New Testament itself. Probably even those who could not master the textbook material could benefit from the well planned exercises. The leader would need to prepare carefully to be sure that the exercises were effective.

The videos effectively introduce visual images and clarify the material. Those on the Resurrection and on Christology are particularly well done and might also be useful in contexts other than this program. The video on Mark includes a moving film of a Latin American base community applying a gospel passage to their lives. On controversial issues, acceptable scholarly positions are always offered, but the student is not always alerted to the existence of differing opinions.

This is an extremely well designed program, successfully balancing prayer, study, and contemporary application. It is highly recommended for any group where both leader and participants are willing to do the necessary preparatory work.

See: Paulist Bible Study Program, p. 221

1.	Up-to-date historical critical scholarship incorporated?	**Yes**
2.	Background information emphasized?	**Yes**
3.	Application to personal and family life emphasized?	**No**
4.	Application to the life and mission of the church included?	**Yes**
5.	Application to broader social issues included?	**Yes**

6. Sexist language avoided?   **Yes**

7. Guidance for prayer at group meetings provided?   **Yes**

8. Discussion questions provided?   **Yes**

9. Practical directions for group leaders provided?   **Yes**

10. Biblical background for group leaders provided?   **Yes**

11. Biblical background for group members presumed?   **No**

12. Participants required to prepare for each session?   **Yes**

JESUS IS LORD! A BASIC CHRISTOLOGY FOR ADULTS.

Thomas Zanzig. St. Mary's Press, 1982. imprimatur. 207 pp., 6 x 9. $7.95. 11 sessions.

This is a textbook for a course on Christology, based mainly on the Gospels. The chapters present very basic material on: The Gospels as testimonies of faith, Jesus' Jewish roots, the world in which Jesus lived, the beginning of Jesus' mission, the kingdom of God, the sayings and parables, the miracles, the death and resurrection, and "Jesus Christ and the Church Through History." This is a program of study about the gospels, not of the gospels. The particular impact of the individual evangelists is inevitably lost in this generalized approach.

Discussion questions at the end of each chapter call participants to personalize the message. In some cases, these questions require reading of actual parts of scripture.

A leader with theological and biblical background would be needed for this program to be fully effective.

1.	Up-to-date historical critical scholarship incorporated?	**Yes**
2.	Background information emphasized?	**Yes**
3.	Application to personal and family life emphasized?	**Yes**
4.	Application to the life and mission of the church included?	**Yes**
5.	Application to broader social issues included?	**Yes**
6.	Sexist language avoided?	**Yes**
7.	Guidance for prayer at group meetings provided?	**No**
8.	Discussion questions provided?	**Yes**
9.	Practical directions for group leaders provided?	**No**
10.	Biblical background for group leaders provided?	**No**
11.	Biblical background for group members presumed?	**No**
12.	Participants required to prepare for each session?	**Yes**

New Testament

JESUS: MYSTERY AND SURPRISE.
AN INTRODUCTION TO THE STUDY OF THE GOSPELS.

Gideon Goosen and Margaret Tomlinson. Published by E.J.Dwyer in Australia, 1989, but available in the U.S. from Morehouse. imprimatur. 50 pp., 6 ½ x 9 ½. $9.95. 6 chapters.

This book seems primarily designed for personal study. It is an introduction to contemporary gospel scholarship. A great deal of information is provided, and varieties of scholarly opinion are often indicated. This is fairly heavy reading, with no emphasis on application.

The particular strength of the book is the 68 exercises suggested throughout. If readers actually stop to do these exercises at the point where they are recommended they will have an excellent introduction to the gospels. Some exercises are: "What Matthean preoccupations do the following references suggest...?" "Read again the Emmaus story and trace the pattern of Eucharistic celebration in the structure and imagery of the story."

Among the exercises a few are recommended for discussion (e.g. "One hears of miracles at Medugorje where rosary beads are turned to gold. What is your reaction to such reports? What place did miracles play in the preaching of Jesus?" "Write down your favorite image of Jesus. Do you know how you came to settle on this image? What incidents in the Gospels give validity to your image of Jesus?")

The final chapter is on the development of Christian creeds, from the New Testament, through the early councils, to some contemporary examples. Appendices include a glossary, a bibliography, and the Instruction on the Historical Truth of the Gospels approved by Pope Paul VI.

A Bible study group could use this book if each participant did the serious study required. The leader would have to organize the program in advance and decide how much material would be covered each week and which exercises would be discussed.

1.	Up-to-date historical critical scholarship incorporated?	**Yes**
2.	Background information emphasized?	**Yes**
3.	Application to personal and family life emphasized?	**No**
4.	Application to the life and mission of the church included?	**Yes**

---

5. Application to broader social issues included?   **Yes**

6. Sexist language avoided?   **No**

7. Guidance for prayer at group meetings provided?   **No**

8. Discussion questions provided?   **Yes**

9. Practical directions for group leaders provided?   **No**

10. Biblical background for group leaders provided?   **No**

11. Biblical background for group members presumed?   **No**

12. Participants required to prepare for each session?   **Yes**

New Testament

THE LIVING GOSPELS.

De Sales Program. Franciscan Communications, 1988. imprimatur. Four video tapes, each containing two sessions, one hour each, Facilitator's Guide, one Participant Manual: $385. Each additional Participant Manual, 137 pp., 8 ½ x 11: $6.50. 8 sessions.

These videos maintain the usual high caliber of the De Sales Program, using pictures effectively to maintain viewer interest. To what extent they succeed in accomplishing their goal of showing the connection between art and theology could be debated. As usual, visual aids are used to present some interesting though trivial material, such as the makeup of the Greek and Hebrew alphabets. Only one visual aid was misleading: a chart which seemed to indicate that Mark utilized material from Q.

The videos are marred by substantial attention given to the Shroud of Turin during the presentations on Mark and John. They were evidently prepared before the carbon dating of the relic. An attempt at updating is made by inserting a written announcement which is quite confusing, claiming that the Shroud is of interest despite the results of the carbon dating, but not explaining in what way. To avoid misleading participants, some groups may wish to use only the segments on Matthew and Luke. The Matthew segment is particularly good in any case.

The lectures integrate Catholic tradition strongly into their presentations (e.g. the Rosary, saints, liturgical year). There is a particularly strong emphasis on application to social issues in the Luke segment.

A positive attitude is expressed toward Judaism, but one speaker's reference to "Jews for Jesus" as a "nice ecumenical bridge" shows an insensitivity to the significance this group has for the vast majority of Jews.

The Participant Manual is very well done, with several informative charts and well selected articles for follow up reading. It asks participants to spend 10 to 15 minutes a day throughout the program reflecting on assigned gospel readings, and provides two questions a day to aid this reflection. One week participants meditate on the beatitudes, one week on the Magnificat, one week on the parables, etc. Participants who follow these suggestions will receive a fine formation in biblical prayer.

See: De Sales Program, p. 211

1. Up-to-date historical critical scholarship incorporated?   **Yes**

2. Background information emphasized?   **Yes**

3. Application to personal and family life emphasized?   **Yes**

4. Application to the life and mission of the church included?   **Yes**

5. Application to broader social issues included?   **Yes**

6. Sexist language avoided?   **Yes**

7. Guidance for prayer at group meetings provided?   **Yes**

8. Discussion questions provided?   **Yes**

9. Practical directions for group leaders provided?   **Yes**

10. Biblical background for group leaders provided?   **No**

11. Biblical background for group members presumed?   **No**

12. Participants required to prepare for each session?   **No**

MARY: A FOUR-SESSION SMALL GROUP BIBLE STUDY ON THE MOTHER OF JESUS.

Edith A. Reuss. Small-Group Bible Study. Augsburg, 1978. 16 pp., 5 ½ x 8 ¼. $.90.

Catholics will welcome this effort from a Lutheran publisher to find in the gospels a common basis on which both Catholics and Protestants can reflect on Mary. Participants read the New Testament passages on Mary and respond to questions which call on them to draw out the implications of the texts, often using imagination to fill in what is not stated. The approach is like much Catholic devotion. It does not utilize contemporary scholarly study of the infancy narratives.

The only problem for a Catholic is one question which is framed to lead anyone without scholarly background to think that the expression "first born son" applied to Jesus implies that Mary had other children. One might also regret the absence of Catholic publications in the books suggested for further study.

Overall, this is a welcome indication that Mary need not be a source of division among Christians. Fortunately, it is also available in Spanish.

See: **Small Group Bible Study, p. 227**

1.	Up-to-date historical critical scholarship incorporated?	**No**
2.	Background information emphasized?	**No**
3.	Application to personal and family life emphasized?	**Yes**
4.	Application to the life and mission of the church included?	**Yes**
5.	Application to broader social issues included?	**Yes**
6.	Sexist language avoided?	**Yes**
7.	Guidance for prayer at group meetings provided?	**Yes**
8.	Discussion questions provided?	**Yes**
9.	Practical directions for group leaders provided?	**No**
10.	Biblical background for group leaders provided?	**No**
11.	Biblical background for group members presumed?	**No**
12.	Participants required to prepare for each session?	**Yes**

ONE TO WATCH, ONE TO PRAY:
A DEVOTIONAL INTRODUCTION TO THE GOSPELS.
Minka Shura Sprague. Morehouse, 1985. 93 pp., 5 x 7 ½. $6.95. 6 sessions.

The title of this book is taken from a child's prayer asking for the protection of the evangelists through the night. The approach is devotional in the very best way, expressing a deep sense of belonging to the family of God which reaches back to Abraham and of the living power of its traditions. The technical jargon of scholarship rarely appears. The author writes with charm and a light touch.

The author was strengthened by her Episcopalian piety through her own childhood and the raising of her family. Later she entered the world of New Testament scholarship, and she is now Professor of New Testament and Biblical Languages at New York Theological Seminary. This apparently simple book is a remarkable synthesis of her own devotional background and contemporary literary criticism of the Gospels.

She avoids such issues as authorship. Instead, in quite masterly fashion she sketches the shapes of the gospels and the special characteristics of each. Each of her chapters would provide a fine preparation for a person reading one of the gospels for the first time and wanting to get a basic feel for it without getting bogged down in technical questions.

The text does not attempt to spell out how the gospels are to be applied to life today, but the reflective questions at the back of the book encourage participants to relate the text to their personal experience.

1.	Up-to-date historical critical scholarship incorporated?	**Yes**
2.	Background information emphasized?	**Yes**
3.	Application to personal and family life emphasized?	**No**
4.	Application to the life and mission of the church included?	**Yes**
5.	Application to broader social issues included?	**No**
6.	Sexist language avoided?	**Yes**
7.	Guidance for prayer at group meetings provided?	**No**
8.	Discussion questions provided?	**Yes**

9. Practical directions for group leaders provided?   **No**

10. Biblical background for group leaders provided?   **No**

11. Biblical background for group members presumed?   **No**

12. Participants required to prepare for each session?   **Yes**

PARABLES.

Daphne D. Hamborg. Friendship Bible Study Series. Augsburg, 1987. Study Book: 8 pp., 5 ½ x 8 ½. $2.85. Leader Guide: 32 pp., 5 ½ x 8 ½. $3.10. 8 sessions.

Each session studies one of these parables: the sower, the pearl of great price, the vineyard laborers, the 10 bridesmaids, the mustard seed, the wicked tenants, the lost coin, the prodigal son. The parables are allowed to serve their function of opening up reflection on many aspects of participants' lives. This is good discussion material for faith sharing groups.

See: Friendship Bible Study Series, p. 215

1.	Up-to-date historical critical scholarship incorporated?	**Yes**
2.	Background information emphasized?	**No**
3.	Application to personal and family life emphasized?	**Yes**
4.	Application to the life and mission of the church included?	**Yes**
5.	Application to broader social issues included?	**Yes**
6.	Sexist language avoided?	**Yes**
7.	Guidance for prayer at group meetings provided?	**Yes**
8.	Discussion questions provided?	**Yes**
9.	Practical directions for group leaders provided?	**Yes**
10.	Biblical background for group leaders provided?	**Yes**
11.	Biblical background for group members presumed?	**No**
12.	Participants required to prepare for each session?	**Yes**

ROLLING BACK THE ROCK.

John Shea. ACTA Publications, 1990. Video tape with 16 page discussion guide. $49.95. 2 to 4 sessions.

Father John Shea's many fans will welcome this video tape of him delivering four classroom lectures in his usual lively style. The first lecture is an introduction to the Passion and Resurrection accounts in the Gospels; the second concerns the events of Holy Thursday, the third those of Good Friday, and the fourth those of Holy Saturday and Easter. These are sophisticated theological reflections, suitable for theologically advanced groups. Beginners would be unable to distinguish between the scholarly background of the material and the poetic license with which Father Shea presents the material. Sexist language is avoided; God is never referred to as masculine.

Each talk is about half an hour, and three discussion questions are provided to assist in applying the message in each talk to the participants' lives. Many groups would not be able to discuss these questions for more than 15 minutes, so leaders may prefer to use two talks per session. There is no suggestion that participants read the relevant scripture passages, but a leader might prepare such suggestions.

1.	Up-to-date historical critical scholarship incorporated?	**Yes**
2.	Background information emphasized?	**No**
3.	Application to personal and family life emphasized?	**Yes**
4.	Application to the life and mission of the church included?	**Yes**
5.	Application to broader social issues included?	**Yes**
6.	Sexist language avoided?	**Yes**
7.	Guidance for prayer at group meetings provided?	**No**
8.	Discussion questions provided?	**Yes**
9.	Practical directions for group leaders provided?	**No**
10.	Biblical background for group leaders provided?	**No**
11.	Biblical background for group members presumed?	**Yes**
12.	Participants required to prepare for each session?	**No**

ISUALIZING SCRIPTURE.
ethren House, 1990. 44 pp., 8 ½ x 11. $8.50. 29 sessions.

his book contains visualizations and reflection questions for use by individuals or
oups wishing to pray over the scripture. Participants should spend 20 to 30
inutes daily reflecting over the brief scripture passage for the week. When the
oup gathers, they share insights from their personal prayer and enter prayerfully
to the visualization and reflection questions provided. Group time is spent in
urnaling and in sharing.

is not necessary to go through the book consecutively. Any one of the visualizations
ight be used separately, perhaps as a time of prayer before a meeting or class. Or
ey could be done in segments by theme. There are eight visualizations on "call,"
ur on "comfort," five on "healing," five on "prayer," seven on "women." Except
or one on Moses at the burning bush, all are from the gospels.

nly the leader would need a copy of the book. This program requires a leader
omfortable leading others in prayer. No particular biblical background is needed
or either leader or participants.

hese are highly recommended for groups seriously interested in developing their
rayer lives and willing to spend quiet time alone and in a group and to share their
piritual journeys.

ee: **Involving Adults in the Bible, p. 125**

1. Up-to-date historical critical scholarship incorporated?	**No**	
2. Background information emphasized?	**No**	
3. Application to personal and family life emphasized?	**Yes**	
4. Application to the life and mission of the church included?	·**Yes**	
5. Application to broader social issues included?	**Yes**	
6. Sexist language avoided?	**Yes**	
7. Guidance for prayer at group meetings provided?	**Yes**	
8. Discussion questions provided?	**Yes**	

9. Practical directions for group leaders provided?   **Yes**

10. Biblical background for group leaders provided?   **No**

11. Biblical background for group members presumed?   **No**

12. Participants required to prepare for each session?   **Yes**

HE GOSPEL OF MATTHEW.

illiam A. Anderson. Benziger New Testament Study Series. Benziger, 1988.
iprimatur. 149 pp., 5 x 8 ¼. $4.68.

iis is a commentary on the Gospel of Matthew in eight chapters. It states that the
ispel of Matthew was written for converts from Judaism, a position which some
holars today would broaden to include Gentiles. However, in general Father
nderson's teaching is, as usual, quite in keeping with the most current scholarship.

ie: **Benziger New Testament Study Series.**, p. 205

1.	Up-to-date historical critical scholarship incorporated?	**Yes**
2.	Background information emphasized?	**Yes**
3.	Application to personal and family life emphasized?	**Yes**
4.	Application to the life and mission of the church included?	**Yes**
5.	Application to broader social issues included?	**No**
6.	Sexist language avoided?	**Yes**
7.	Guidance for prayer at group meetings provided?	**No**
8.	Discussion questions provided?	**Yes**
9.	Practical directions for group leaders provided?	**No**
10.	Biblical background for group leaders provided?	**No**
11.	Biblical background for group members presumed?	**No**
12.	Participants required to prepare for each session?	**Yes**

New Testament

---

* QUESTIONS OF CHRISTIANS: VOL. 2, MATTHEW'S RESPONSE.

John C. Massion and Helen Reichert Lambin. ACTA Publications, 1984. imprimatur. 3 audio tapes and booklet, 138 pp., 5 ¼ x 8 ¼. $29.95. Each additional booklet, $3.95. 9 sessions.

The introductory tape segments in this program are particularly creative. Each is a lively dramatization of conversation among members of Matthew's community. The dramatizations make the first century Christians very human, people we can smile at and identify with. This is a very effective way to bring to life the issues with which Matthew was dealing. Regretfully, no women are shown as participating in the life of the Matthean community. Nevertheless, the tapes are very well done and could be useful also for other classes on Matthew or on the early church.

Wisely, the commentary admits the variety of scholarly opinions on the structure of Matthew without going into detail about them.

As one might expect in a study of Matthew, the discussion questions about the church are particularly good.

See: Questions of Christians, p. 223

1.	Up-to-date historical critical scholarship incorporated?	Yes
2.	Background information emphasized?	No
3.	Application to personal and family life emphasized?	Yes
4.	Application to the life and mission of the church included?	Yes
5.	Application to broader social issues included?	No
6.	Sexist language avoided?	Yes
7.	Guidance for prayer at group meetings provided?	Yes
8.	Discussion questions provided?	Yes
9.	Practical directions for group leaders provided?	Yes
10.	Biblical background for group leaders provided?	No

---

11. Biblical background for group members presumed?   **No**

12. Participants required to prepare for each session?   **No**

SERMON ON THE MOUNT.

Robert C. Bowman. Covenant Bible Studies. Brethren Press, 1988. 40 pp., 8 ½ x 5 ½. $2.95. 10 sessions.

This program challenges participants to apply the Sermon on the Mount to their personal and church community lives, and also to national and global issues. There is little academic analysis of the text, but many insights about its relevance to real issues of today. The difficulties of application are not glossed over or resolved in a simplistic way but opened up for discussion.

For each session participants are asked to prepare by reading a brief passage from the Sermon on the Mount. Directions are given on how to reflect on its relationship to their lives. There are also three-and-a-half pages of reflection to be read. However, persons who had not prepared could probably participate in the discussion.

See: Covenant Bible Studies, p. 209

1.	Up-to-date historical critical scholarship incorporated?	**Yes**
2.	Background information emphasized?	**No**
3.	Application to personal and family life emphasized?	**Yes**
4.	Application to the life and mission of the church included?	**Yes**
5.	Application to broader social issues included?	**Yes**
6.	Sexist language avoided?	**Yes**
7.	Guidance for prayer at group meetings provided?	**No**
8.	Discussion questions provided?	**Yes**
9.	Practical directions for group leaders provided?	**No**
10.	Biblical background for group leaders provided?	**No**
11.	Biblical background for group members presumed?	**No**
12.	Participants required to prepare for each session?	**Yes**

THE GOSPEL OF MARK.

William A. Anderson. Benziger New Testament Study Series. Benziger, 1988. Imprimatur. 111 pp., 5 ¼ x 8. $4.68

This commentary on Mark is divided into 25 segments, about four pages each.

See: **Benziger New Testament Study Series, p. 205**

1.	Up-to-date historical critical scholarship incorporated?	**Yes**
2.	Background information emphasized?	**Yes**
3.	Application to personal and family life emphasized?	**Yes**
4.	Application to the life and mission of the church included?	**Yes**
5.	Application to broader social issues included?	**Yes**
6.	Sexist language avoided?	**Yes**
7.	Guidance for prayer at group meetings provided?	**No**
8.	Discussion questions provided?	**Yes**
9.	Practical directions for group leaders provided?	**No**
10.	Biblical background for group leaders provided?	**No**
11.	Biblical background for group members presumed?	**No**
12.	Participants required to prepare for each session?	**Yes**

QUESTIONS OF CHRISTIANS: VOLUME 1, MARK'S RESPONSE.

John C. Massion and Helen Reichert Lambin. ACTA Publications, 1980. imprimatur. 2 audio tapes and booklet, 94 pp., 5 ¼ x 8 ¼. $19.95. Each additional booklet, $3.95. 3 sessions.

The audio segments of this first of the Questions of Christians series are quite different from later ones. Each audio has first a segment on group dynamics for the guidance and encouragement of the leader. This is followed by two segments to be played for the group, both providing background information on Mark. While the material on group dynamics is good, this may not be the most practical form for presenting it. The two segments of input are less conducive to the sharing process than the more right brain segments which introduce the Matthew, Luke and John programs.

The traditional view that Mark was written for the Christians in Rome is followed, though some scholars today question it.

See: Questions of Christians, p. 223

1.	Up-to-date historical critical scholarship incorporated?	**Yes**
2.	Background information emphasized?	**No**
3.	Application to personal and family life emphasized?	**Yes**
4.	Application to the life and mission of the church included?	**Yes**
5.	Application to broader social issues included?	**No**
6.	Sexist language avoided?	**Yes**
7.	Guidance for prayer at group meetings provided?	**Yes**
8.	Discussion questions provided?	**Yes**
9.	Practical directions for group leaders provided?	**Yes**
10.	Biblical background for group leaders provided?	**No**
11.	Biblical background for group members presumed?	**No**
12.	Participants required to prepare for each session?	**No**

BREAKING OPEN THE GOSPEL OF LUKE.

Gerard P. Weber and Robert Miller. St.Anthony Messenger Press, 1990. imprimatur. 101 pp., 5 ½ x 8 ½. $5.95. 6 or 7 sessions.

This is not the usual type of study of Luke's gospel. Instead of progressing in order through the gospel, each chapter uses as starting points real issues of people's lives such as: personal identity and vocation, sin and reconciliation, phases of the faith journey, the Eucharist, the church, social justice. Appropriate stories from Luke's gospel are brought in as a means of reflecting on these issues.

Stories are selected from the infancy narrative, parables, healing stories, and meal stories. The Emmaus story receives particular attention, and the Martha and Mary story carries surprising insight. Enough background information is provided to enable participants to explore the stories with new glasses to see how they express realities which are part of everyday life.

Scattered through each chapter at appropriate spots are reflection questions, some which encourage reflection directly on participants' own lives, others which find parallels between a Lukan story and their lives. The questions are open-ended and show sensitivity to real concerns of ordinary Catholics. Some of them require the sharing of personal religious experience, doubts, etc.

Participants would need to read the chapter (about 12 pages), look up the scripture references in their Bibles, and answer the questions in preparation for each session. If they do so, lively and enriching discussion can be expected.

Though the emphasis is more on application than on study, this book makes clear why our reading of scripture should be guided by scholarship. The influence of contemporary scholarship can be detected in the background at several places, especially in the fine explanation of parables.

Catholic church documents are quoted and much concern is shown for Catholic issues.

This is not a technical nor particularly difficult book. It requires mainly an ability and willingness to reflect on one's own life. It is full of fresh insights which will be valuable for both beginning and advanced students of scripture. It will therefore be ideal for the many groups which include people at very different levels.

1. Up-to-date historical critical scholarship incorporated? **Yes**

2. Background information emphasized? **No**

3. Application to personal and family life emphasized?   **Yes**

4. Application to the life and mission of the church included?   **Yes**

5. Application to broader social issues included?   **Yes**

6. Sexist language avoided?   **Yes**

7. Guidance for prayer at group meetings provided?   **No**

8. Discussion questions provided?   **Yes**

9. Practical directions for group leaders provided?   **No**

10. Biblical background for group leaders provided?   **No**

11. Biblical background for group members presumed?   **No**

12. Participants required to prepare for each session?   **Yes**

THE GOSPEL OF LUKE.
William A. Anderson. Benziger New Testament Study Series. Benziger, 1988. imprimatur. 137 pp., 5 ¼ x 8. $4.68.

This is a commentary on the Gospel of Luke in eight chapters. It states that the unique quality of Luke is that he shows Jesus intending his message to reach out to all peoples.

See: Benziger New Testament Study Series, p. 205

1. Up-to-date historical critical scholarship incorporated?   **Yes**

2. Background information emphasized?   **Yes**

3. Application to personal and family life emphasized?   **Yes**

4. Application to the life and mission of the church included?   **Yes**

5. Application to broader social issues included?   **No**

6. Sexist language avoided?   **Yes**

7. Guidance for prayer at group meetings provided?   **No**

8. Discussion questions provided?   **Yes**

9. Practical directions for group leaders provided?   **No**

10. Biblical background for group leaders provided?   **No**

11. Biblical background for group members presumed?   **No**

12. Participants required to prepare for each session?   **Yes**

New Testament

Luke

QUESTIONS OF CHRISTIANS: VOL. 3, LUKE'S RESPONSE.
John C. Massion and Helen Reichert Lambin. ACTA Publications, 1985. imprimatur. 3 audio tapes and booklet, 138 pp., 5 ¼ x 8 ¼. $29.95. Each additional booklet, $3.95. 8 sessions.

The themes explored in Luke's gospel are: the Spirit, journey, mercy and forgiveness, social justice and peace, miracles and healing, prayer, Eucharist and meals. Luke's gospel is shown to mirror a time of transition in his community and therefore to have a message for today's transition times.

The introductory tape segment for each session is a story, poem, or song planned to help participants enter into the experience which is the basis for the study. Sources are extremely varied, including Charles Dickens, a newspaper story, a rabbinic tale, and Robert Frost. All are well chosen to help participants get into their own experience as the point of view from which to read Luke. The second tape segments giving scholarly background on Luke are very brief.

See: Questions of Christians, p. 223

1.	Up-to-date historical critical scholarship incorporated?	Yes
2.	Background information emphasized?	No
3.	Application to personal and family life emphasized?	Yes
4.	Application to the life and mission of the church included?	Yes
5.	Application to broader social issues included?	Yes
6.	Sexist language avoided?	Yes
7.	Guidance for prayer at group meetings provided?	Yes
8.	Discussion questions provided?	Yes
9.	Practical directions for group leaders provided?	Yes
10.	Biblical background for group leaders provided?	No
11.	Biblical background for group members presumed?	No
12.	Participants required to prepare for each session?	No

For another program on Luke, see Beginners' Guide to Bible Sharing, Vol.II, p. 107

Picking the "Right" Bible Study Program   © 1992 ACTA Publications   159

New Testament

THE GOSPEL OF JOHN.
William A. Anderson. Benziger New Testament Study Series. Benziger, 1988. imprimatur. 118 pp., 5 ¼ x 8. $4.68.

This is a commentary on the Gospel of John in eight chapters.

See: Benziger New Testament Study Series, p. 205

1. Up-to-date historical critical scholarship incorporated?	**Yes**
2. Background information emphasized?	**Yes**
3. Application to personal and family life emphasized?	**Yes**
4. Application to the life and mission of the church included?	**Yes**
5. Application to broader social issues included?	**No**
6. Sexist language avoided?	**Yes**
7. Guidance for prayer at group meetings provided?	**No**
8. Discussion questions provided?	**Yes**
9. Practical directions for group leaders provided?	**No**
10. Biblical background for group leaders provided?	**No**
11. Biblical background for group members presumed?	**No**
12. Participants required to prepare for each session?	**Yes**

New Testament

QUESTIONS OF CHRISTIANS: VOLUME 4, JOHN'S RESPONSE.

Helen Reichert Lambin. ACTA Publications, 1986. imprimatur. 3 audio tapes and booklet, 150 pp., 5 ¼ x 8 ¼, $29.95. Each additional booklet, $3.95. 8 sessions.

This program studies the one basic question in John, "Who is Jesus?" The emphasis on personal religious experience is greater than in the other programs in this series, as is to be expected in a study of John.

There is strong emphasis on the difference between John and the synoptics, and this program would probably be best for groups which have studied the synoptics. The information provided links the evangelist rather more closely with John the Apostle than recent scholarship does.

For the first session, the introductory tape segment is a very interesting discussion about the church among a group of first century Christians from various communities. It effectively dramatizes how different the Johannine Christians are from others. For the following sessions, the introductory tape segments are accounts of personal experiences of Jesus by contemporary Christians. They are from a variety of ordinary people and are well suited to initiating sharing of the personal experience of group members.

See: Questions of Christians, p. 223

1.	Up-to-date historical critical scholarship incorporated?	**Yes**
2.	Background information emphasized?	**No**
3.	Application to personal and family life emphasized?	**Yes**
4.	Application to the life and mission of the church included?	**Yes**
5.	Application to broader social issues included?	**Yes**
6.	Sexist language avoided?	**Yes**
7.	Guidance for prayer at group meetings provided?	**Yes**
8.	Discussion questions provided?	**Yes**
9.	Practical directions for group leaders provided?	**Yes**
10.	Biblical background for group leaders provided?	**No**

---

11. Biblical background for group members presumed?   **No**

12. Participants required to prepare for each session?   **No**

THE ACTS OF THE APOSTLES.

William A. Anderson. Benziger New Testament Study Series. Benziger, 1988. Imprimatur. 131 pp., 5 ¼ x 8. $4.68.

This is an easy to read commentary on an interesting part of scripture. It would be a good starting point for anyone wishing to try the Benziger series for group use.

See: **Benziger New Testament Study Series.**, p. 205

1. Up-to-date historical critical scholarship incorporated?	**Yes**
2. Background information emphasized?	**Yes**
3. Application to personal and family life emphasized?	**Yes**
4. Application to the life and mission of the church included?	**Yes**
5. Application to broader social issues included?	**No**
6. Sexist language avoided?	**Yes**
7. Guidance for prayer at group meetings provided?	**No**
8. Discussion questions provided?	**Yes**
9. Practical directions for group leaders provided?	**No**
10. Biblical background for group leaders provided?	**No**
11. Biblical background for group members presumed?	**No**
12. Participants required to prepare for each session?	**Yes**

New Testament

THE ACTS OF THE APOSTLES.

Little Rock. Liturgical Press, 1983. imprimatur. Study Set (Study Guide 32 pp., 5 ¼ x 8 ¼ and Collegeville Bible Commentary by William S. Kurz, S.J., 109 pp., 5 ¼ x 8 ¼) $5.25. Answer Guide, 7 pp., 5 ¼ x 8 ¼, $1.00. Ten audio lectures (on 5 cassettes) $30.00. Ten video lectures (on 2 cassettes) $95.00. 10 sessions.

This is recommended as the first unit for groups using the Little Rock Program. The questions and lectures are geared to beginners.

The program can be used with or without the taped lectures. These lectures apply the main themes of Acts to today. They express a strong sense of church and of the call to evangelization. They are easily understood and generally accurate, but lack spark. This is a gentle introduction, not a challenging program.

See: Little Rock Scripture Study Program, p. 217

1.	Up-to-date historical critical scholarship incorporated?	**Yes**
2.	Background information emphasized?	**Yes**
3.	Application to personal and family life emphasized?	**Yes**
4.	Application to the life and mission of the church included?	**Yes**
5.	Application to broader social issues included?	**Yes**
6.	Sexist language avoided?	**Yes**
7.	Guidance for prayer at group meetings provided?	**Yes**
8.	Discussion questions provided?	**Yes**
9.	Practical directions for group leaders provided?	**Yes**
10.	Biblical background for group leaders provided?	**No**
11.	Biblical background for group members presumed?	**No**
12.	Participants required to prepare for each session?	**Yes**

For other programs on Acts, see: Beginners' Guide to Bible Sharing, Vol.I, p. 105 and Acts-Paul's Early and Great Letters, p. 169

ACTS-PAUL'S EARLY AND GREAT LETTERS.

Mary Mauren. Scripture Share and Prayer, 1982. 12 audio tapes, 60 minutes each, and loose-leaf manual with study guides which may be reproduced. $75. 12 sessions.

This program provides a one session overview of the New Testament, and covers 1 and 2 Thessalonians, Galatians, 1 and 2 Corinthians (3 sessions), and Romans (6 sessions). Acts is not studied explicitly, but passages relevant to the letters are summarized in the lectures.

The rapid overview of the New Testament in the first lecture may be more overwhelming than helpful for some groups. It may also be repetitious for groups which have recently completed *Scripture Foundations* in this program. Some groups may want to omit it or use it as a conclusion instead of an introduction.

Both assignment questions and lectures are on the level of serious study. Contemporary scholarship is generally represented, though many scholars would disagree with the speaker's certainty that 2 Thessalonians is by Paul.

Useful handouts are provided, including a list of key terms (with definitions) used in Romans .

Some lectures are purely informational; others include sometimes lengthy sharings from Mary Mauren's personal experience. Considerable attention is given to issues of concern to Catholics raised in the pre-Vatican II church and still trying to adjust to the new era.

This is a good program for advanced groups wanting to get into the meat of the Pauline letters.

See: **Scripture Share and Prayer, p. 225**

1. Up-to-date historical critical scholarship incorporated?	**Yes**	
2. Background information emphasized?	**Yes**	
3. Application to personal and family life emphasized?	**Yes**	
4. Application to the life and mission of the church included?	**Yes**	
5. Application to broader social issues included?	**Yes**	
6. Sexist language avoided?	**Yes**	

7. Guidance for prayer at group meetings provided?   **No**

8. Discussion questions provided?   **Yes**

9. Practical directions for group leaders provided?   **No**

10. Biblical background for group leaders provided?   **No**

11. Biblical background for group members presumed?   **Yes**

12. Participants required to prepare for each session?   **Yes**

New Testament

---

* THE APOSTLE PAUL:
MALE CHAUVINIST OR PROPONENT OF EQUALITY?

Philip A. Cunningham. Hi-Time, 1986. imprimatur. 24 pp., 8 ½ x 11. $4.25 ($2.95 if five or more copies are ordered). 6 sessions.

This is a very well planned adult inquiry guide. Each chapter gives one or two pages of relevant background, then instructs participants to look up certain passages from Paul and answer questions aimed at clarifying his attitude toward women. The inquirer is inevitably led to see that Paul is much less of a chauvinist than generally imagined.

The author says that participants should do the work as preparation for the session, but some groups might want to do it during the first part of the session. The preparatory work is not likely to take more than an hour, nor is the discussion likely to take more than another hour. This could be a very practical program for lunch hour groups or groups which want to give only forty five minutes or an hour of their meeting time to Bible study.

This program meets a great need for those who are troubled about women's role in the church and particularly Paul's position on this question. At the same time, its easy style and interesting outcome will whet the appetite of beginners for further Bible study. More experienced Bible students will find it interesting because of the unusual material presented.

1. Up-to-date historical critical scholarship incorporated?	**Yes**
2. Background information emphasized?	**Yes**
3. Application to personal and family life emphasized?	**No**
4. Application to the life and mission of the church included?	**Yes**
5. Application to broader social issues included?	**Yes**
6. Sexist language avoided?	**Yes**
7. Guidance for prayer at group meetings provided?	**No**
8. Discussion questions provided?	**Yes**
9. Practical directions for group leaders provided?	**No**

---

10. Biblical background for group leaders provided?   **No**

11. Biblical background for group members presumed?   **No**

12. Participants required to prepare for each session?   **Yes**

RST AND SECOND CORINTHIANS.
illiam A. Anderson. Benziger New Testament Study Series. Benziger, 1988.
primatur. 115 pp., 5 ¼ x 8. $4.68.

is book consists of one chapter of introduction to 1 Corinthians, and four of
mmentary on it, and one chapter of introduction to 2 Corinthians and five of
mmentary on it. The letters are shown to give a unique picture of the early Christian
mmunity as it struggled to throw off its pagan attitudes and practices. Paul is
own to deal with the Corinthians in the loving, though sometimes exasperated,
ay in which parents deal with their children.

e: **Benziger New Testament Study Series, p. 205**

1. Up-to-date historical critical scholarship incorporated?	**Yes**
2. Background information emphasized?	**Yes**
3. Application to personal and family life emphasized?	**Yes**
4. Application to the life and mission of the church included?	**Yes**
5. Application to broader social issues included?	**No**
6. Sexist language avoided?	**Yes**
7. Guidance for prayer at group meetings provided?	**No**
8. Discussion questions provided?	**Yes**
9. Practical directions for group leaders provided?	**No**
10. Biblical background for group leaders provided?	**No**
11. Biblical background for group members presumed?	**No**
12. Participants required to prepare for each session?	**Yes**

AND 2 CORINTHIANS.

mes A. Dumke. Men's Bible Study Series. Augsburg, 1988. Study Book: 48 pp.,
½ x 9 ½. $2.85. Leader Guide: 32 pp., 4 ½ x 9 ½. $3.10. 10 sessions.

ach half hour session deals with a brief selected passage from 1 or 2 Corinthians.
articipants learn that the Corinthian congregation was much like modern ones, so
uch of Paul's message to the Corinthians is applicable today. Like 1 and 2
orinthians itself does, the sessions deal with a variety of topics, from charitable
ving to love to the resurrection.

ee: **Men's Bible Study Series, p. 219**

1. Up-to-date historical critical scholarship incorporated?	**Yes**
2. Background information emphasized?	**No**
3. Application to personal and family life emphasized?	**Yes**
4. Application to the life and mission of the church included?	**Yes**
5. Application to broader social issues included?	**No**
6. Sexist language avoided?	**Yes**
7. Guidance for prayer at group meetings provided?	**Yes**
8. Discussion questions provided?	**Yes**
9. Practical directions for group leaders provided?	**Yes**
10. Biblical background for group leaders provided?	**Yes**
11. Biblical background for group members presumed?	**No**
12. Participants required to prepare for each session?	**No**

New Testament

1, 2, THESSALONIANS.

Frank W. Klos. Small-Group Bible Study. Augsburg Fortress, 1989. 20 pp., 5 ½ x 8 ¼. $1.05. 5 sessions.

This booklet provides discussion questions for five sessions on 1 and 2 Thessalonians. The final session involves a creative project in which participants compose a creed from material in these two letters.

The introduction states categorically that 2 Thessalonians was written by Paul, a theory with which many scholars would disagree. However, this is not an important issue for the kind of discussion to which this booklet is leading.

See: **Small-Group Bible Study, p. 227**

1.	Up-to-date historical critical scholarship incorporated?	**No**
2.	Background information emphasized?	**No**
3.	Application to personal and family life emphasized?	**Yes**
4.	Application to the life and mission of the church included?	**Yes**
5.	Application to broader social issues included?	**No**
6.	Sexist language avoided?	**Yes**
7.	Guidance for prayer at group meetings provided?	**Yes**
8.	Discussion questions provided?	**Yes**
9.	Practical directions for group leaders provided?	**No**
10.	Biblical background for group leaders provided?	**No**
11.	Biblical background for group members presumed?	**No**
12.	Participants required to prepare for each session?	**Yes**

HEBREWS.

Men's Bible Study Series. Augsburg, 1986. Study Book: 48 pp., 4½ x 9½. $2.85. Leader Guide: 32 pp., 4 ½ x 9 ½. $3.10. 10 sessions.

Each session reflects on a selected passage from Hebrews, showing how this part of scripture explores the heart of Christian faith: Jesus Christ, human and divine, the high priest who reconciles us with the Father. Participants also see how the author of Hebrews intertwines the Old and New Testaments, using the Old Testament in a way very different from that of modern exegesis. Hebrews shows that the kings, priests and prophets of the Old Testament are all leading toward Jesus, who is fully king, priest and prophet. Participants are challenged to share their faith in Jesus with others.

See: **Men's Bible Study Series. p. 219**

1.	Up-to-date historical critical scholarship incorporated?	**Yes**
2.	Background information emphasized?	**No**
3.	Application to personal and family life emphasized?	**Yes**
4.	Application to the life and mission of the church included?	**Yes**
5.	Application to broader social issues included?	**No**
6.	Sexist language avoided?	**Yes**
7.	Guidance for prayer at group meetings provided?	**Yes**
8.	Discussion questions provided?	**Yes**
9.	Practical directions for group leaders provided?	**Yes**
10.	Biblical background for group leaders provided?	**Yes**
11.	Biblical background for group members presumed?	**No**
12.	Participants required to prepare for each session?	**No**

THE PASTORAL LETTERS.

William A. Anderson. Benziger New Testament Study Series. Benziger, 1988. Imprimatur. 95 pp., 5 ¼ x 8. $4.68.

This commentary covers 1 Timothy, 2 Timothy, Titus, and Hebrews in eight segments. These are introduced as letters that reflect the struggles of the early church. Hebrews helped the early Christians to bridge the gap between the old and the new. The Pastorals helped them to adapt to a changing world.

See: **Benziger New Testament Study Series, p. 205**

1.	Up-to-date historical critical scholarship incorporated?	**Yes**
2.	Background information emphasized?	**Yes**
3.	Application to personal and family life emphasized?	**Yes**
4.	Application to the life and mission of the church included?	**Yes**
5.	Application to broader social issues included?	**No**
6.	Sexist language avoided?	**Yes**
7.	Guidance for prayer at group meetings provided?	**No**
8.	Discussion questions provided?	**Yes**
9.	Practical directions for group leaders provided?	**No**
10.	Biblical background for group leaders provided?	**No**
11.	Biblical background for group members presumed?	**No**
12.	Participants required to prepare for each session?	**Yes**

AUL'S EARLY AND PRISON LETTERS.

/illiam A. Anderson. Benziger New Testament Study Series. Benziger, 1988.
nprimatur. 120 pp., 5 ¼ x 8. $4.68.

his commentary covers First Thessalonians, Second Thessalonians, Philippians,
hilemon, Colossians, and Ephesians in 20 segments. Father Anderson is particu-
rly good at presenting clearly the various theories about the authorship of these
tters.

ee: **Benziger New Testament Study Series. p. 205**

1. Up-to-date historical critical scholarship incorporated?	**Yes**
2. Background information emphasized?	**Yes**
3. Application to personal and family life emphasized?	**Yes**
4. Application to the life and mission of the church included?	**Yes**
5. Application to broader social issues included?	**Yes**
6. Sexist language avoided?	**Yes**
7. Guidance for prayer at group meetings provided?	**No**
8. Discussion questions provided?	**Yes**
9. Practical directions for group leaders provided?	**No**
10. Biblical background for group leaders provided?	**No**
11. Biblical background for group members presumed?	**No**
12. Participants required to prepare for each session?	**Yes**

New Testament

PHILIPPIANS, EPHESIANS:
BECOMING A CARING COMMUNITY.
Serendipity Group Bible Study. Serendipity, 1989. 64 pp, 6 ½ x 9. $4.95. 16 to 21 sessions.

This program is intended for groups who do not have time to do homework, and is planned to be suitable for interested persons whether or not they attend any church. While intended primarily for Protestants, it could also be used by Catholics.

There are no detailed lesson plans. Each page contains the three elements provided:
1. The text of a section of the NIV translation of scripture. This is a Protestant translation. No footnotes or cross references are included with it.
2. Discussion questions.
3. On a facing page, a running commentary on the scripture given.

The strength of this program is in the discussion questions. Each page starts with opening questions which serve as ice breakers, a means of sharing personal experience before getting into the text of the scripture (e.g. "When you care for someone, are you more likely to send a funny card or a touching one?" "What New Year's resolution have you been least successful in keeping?") A second group of questions called "Dig" assist in a careful reading of the text. A third group called "Reflect" challenge participants to apply the text to their personal lives. These questions are only slightly different from those in the *Serendipity Bible*.

The running commentary is a selection of points from popular Protestant commentaries. It is not technical and generally not controversial. It does differ from most Catholic and mainline scholars today in insisting that Ephesians was written by Paul, and at one point it interprets a passage in a way with which Catholics will not agree. (It states, without any evidence, that the "helmet of salvation" spoken of in Ephesians is "the sure knowledge that one's salvation is secure--that the outcome of the battle is already known." This seems to imply that it is impossible for salvation to be lost by sin.) There is a particular emphasis on individual words. For instance, we are rather frequently told how often a given word is used in various parts of the Bible. It is not clear how this commentary is meant to be used. It would make dull reading if read aloud in the group. Probably the intent is to have it there in case a question should arise, but the format does not seem the most practical for such use.

In the center of the book is an insert of 16 pages of general advice about group process, titled "Time for a Check-up". This is well put and cleverly illustrated with cartoons. It is the same insert that is found in *1 John, Galatians* and presumably elsewhere.

While this book can certainly be used as it is, a Catholic group wanting to use this program would probably be more satisfied using their own Bibles for the text, which would give them the advantage of easily available information in the footnotes. If a commentary was desired, one such as the *Collegeville Bible Commentary* would be an improvement on the one provided here. Then only the leader would need a copy of the questions and could either take them from this book or from the *Serendipity Bible.*

See: Serendipity Bible, p. 233
Collegeville Bible Commentary, p. 231
1 John, Galatians: Exposing Religious Counterfeits, p. 115

1. Up-to-date historical critical scholarship incorporated? **No**

2. Background information emphasized? **No**

3. Application to personal and family life emphasized? **Yes**

4. Application to the life and mission of the church included? **Yes**

5. Application to broader social issues included? **Yes**

6. Sexist language avoided? **Yes**

7. Guidance for prayer at group meetings provided? **No**

8. Discussion questions provided? **Yes**

9. Practical directions for group leaders provided? **No**

10. Biblical background for group leaders provided? **No**

11. Biblical background for group members presumed? **No**

12. Participants required to prepare for each session? **No**

ROMANS AND GALATIANS.

William A. Anderson. Benziger New Testament Study Series. Benziger, 1988. Imprimatur. 96 pp., 5 ¼ x 8. $4.68.

This commentary gives an introductory chapter each to Romans and Galatians plus six chapters which paraphrase and explain Romans and four which do the same for Galatians.

See: **Benziger New Testament Study Series. p. 205.**

1.	Up-to-date historical critical scholarship incorporated?	**Yes**
2.	Background information emphasized?	**Yes**
3.	Application to personal and family life emphasized?	**Yes**
4.	Application to the life and mission of the church included?	**Yes**
5.	Application to broader social issues included?	**No**
6.	Sexist language avoided?	**Yes**
7.	Guidance for prayer at group meetings provided?	**No**
8.	Discussion questions provided?	**Yes**
9.	Practical directions for group leaders provided?	**No**
10.	Biblical background for group leaders provided?	**No**
11.	Biblical background for group members presumed?	**No**
12.	Participants required to prepare for each session?	**Yes**

New Testament

* THE WRITINGS OF ST.PAUL.

De Sales Program. Franciscan Communications. imprimatur. 4 videos, containing a total of 8 one-hour sessions; One Participant Manual, 114 pp., 8 ½ x 11, One Facilitator's Guide. $385. Additional Participant Manuals, $6.50 each. 8 sessions.

These eight sessions provide a very good introduction to the Pauline letters. No previous knowledge or heavy study is required, though the program will be much more beneficial for those who read the articles provided and do the weekly "faith exercises" suggested.

As usual in this series, material that might be shocking to the uninitiated (e.g. that Paul did not write all the letters attributed to him) is presented gently and persuasively.

Geographical and historical information and relevant passages from Acts are included. The emphasis is more on understanding the communities to which Paul wrote than on theological questions.

Contemporary issues related to the text and of particular interest to Catholics receive considerable attention (e.g. fundamentalist teachings about the end of the world, divorce, annulment, the place of women in the church). Jewish and ecumenical issues are also noted.

This is an easy introduction to a difficult topic.

See: De Sales Program, p. 211

1. Up-to-date historical critical scholarship incorporated?   **Yes**

2. Background information emphasized?   **Yes**

3. Application to personal and family life emphasized?   **Yes**

4. Application to the life and mission of the church included?   **Yes**

5. Application to broader social issues included?   **Yes**

6. Sexist language avoided?   **Yes**

7. Guidance for prayer at group meetings provided?   **Yes**

8. Discussion questions provided?   **Yes**

9. Practical directions for group leaders provided?   Yes

10. Biblical background for group leaders provided?   No

11. Biblical background for group members presumed?   No

12. Participants required to prepare for each session?   No

For another program on Romans, see Beginners' Guide to Bible Sharing, Vol.II, p. 107

1, 2, 3 JOHN.

Nancy Koester. Friendship Bible Study Series. Augsburg, 1986. Study Book: 48 pp., 5 ½ x 8 ½. $2.85. Leader's Guide: 32 pp., 5 ½ x 8 ½. $3.10. 8 sessions.

The Johannine letters are probably not the easiest part of the Bible to use as a basis for group discussion, but a group that does want to use them will find this program most helpful. A sensitivity to ecumenical concerns is evident. The emphasis on building up the small faith community which gathers for these discussions is particularly conspicuous in this program, though it is present in all materials in this series.

See: Friendship Bible Study Series. p. 215

1. Up-to-date historical critical scholarship incorporated?   **Yes**

2. Background information emphasized?   **No**

3. Application to personal and family life emphasized?   **Yes**

4. Application to the life and mission of the church included?   **Yes**

5. Application to broader social issues included?   **Yes**

6. Sexist language avoided?   **Yes**

7. Guidance for prayer at group meetings provided?   **Yes**

8. Discussion questions provided?   **Yes**

9. Practical directions for group leaders provided?   **Yes**

10. Biblical background for group leaders provided?   **Yes**

11. Biblical background for group members presumed?   **No**

12. Participants required to prepare for each session?   **Yes**

1 JOHN.

Lyman Coleman and Richard Peace. Mastering the Basics. Serendipity, 1988. Study Guide: 64 pp, 8 x 9 ½. $5.95. Pastor/Teacher Commentary: 64 pp., 8 x 9 ½. $10.00. 7 or 13 sessions.

The study guide is intended for personal or small group use. The scripture text is the NIV. The commentary is a slightly enlarged version of that in *1 John, Galatians* and presents the same problems. The discussion questions are somewhat more developed than those in *1 John, Galatians* and include a "case study" for each session.

The element found here but not in *1 John, Galatians* is 30-45 minutes of homework for each session in workbook format. This may include multiple choice questions, topical study, paraphrasing exercises, summarizing, composing of prayers, memorizing verses, etc. It always includes application to daily life.

Meetings are to consist of 15 minutes of coffee and announcements, 30-45 minutes of Bible study, and 15 minutes of sharing prayer and prayer requests. If the pastor or teacher is to give a presentation, this is an additional 30-45 minutes, either after the group session or at another time.

Discussion groups should be four persons, with an empty chair to remind everyone of the goal of bringing new people continually into the group. When the group reaches eight, it should split.

The approach starts with a "bird's eye" view of a passage, then moves to a "worm's eye" view by digging deeper, and ends with application to participants' lives.

The Pastor/Teacher Commentary is a guide for a pastor who wants to gather the participants in several small groups for a large group conclusion to each session. It is very well done, with detailed organizational directions for getting such a program started and maintaining it. For each session it gives an orientation, goals and a lesson plan with mini-lectures, questions to ask participants, and answers to be expected from participants--all completely written out. Educational methodology is very good, and should help to wean users away from the straight lecture method.

The main topic, related to the secessionists in 1 John, is modern cults. These include the Unification Church, The Way International, Jim Jones, Bahai, Mormonism, Jehovah's Witness, Scientology, Hare Krishna, etc. Much interesting material is provided about certain cults, showing how they fail to meet the criteria of 1 John for orthodoxy. In struggling to explain how one distinguishes a cult from a church, the authors seem to have no clear criteria other than the Bible. Teachers who believe in the authority of the church would have to expand these ideas.

The presentations also emphasize the responsibility of church members to behave in a way that will draw those currently attracted by cults into their churches. Considerable time is given to teaching how to witness to one's own experience of coming to know Jesus as Lord and Savior. One session encourages small group evangelism by inviting people into one's home.

Teachers may disagree with the statement that "the central fact of human nature is that it is flawed." However, many excellent insights can be found, including some on feminist concerns and some on the tensions between modern American culture and the gospel.

The seven-week plan doubles up material from certain sessions, and does not include the sessions on 2 John and 3 John.

See: 1 John, Galatians, p. 115

1.	Up-to-date historical critical scholarship incorporated?	**No**
2.	Background information emphasized?	**No**
3.	Application to personal and family life emphasized?	**Yes**
4.	Application to the life and mission of the church included?	**Yes**
5.	Application to broader social issues included?	**Yes**
6.	Sexist language avoided?	**Yes**
7.	Guidance for prayer at group meetings provided?	**No**
8.	Discussion questions provided?	**Yes**
9.	Practical directions for group leaders provided?	**Yes**
10.	Biblical background for group leaders provided?	**No**
11.	Biblical background for group members presumed?	**No**
12.	Participants required to prepare for each session?	**Yes**

THE UNIVERSAL LETTERS.

William A. Anderson. Benziger New Testament Study Series. Benziger, 1988. imprimatur. 79 pp., 5 ¼ x 8. $4.68.

This commentary covers the First, Second, and Third Letters of John, the First and Second Letters of Peter, and the Letters of James and Jude, in 11 segments. It is explained that the universal letters, much like a TV sermon today, are addressed to the church in general, not to a particular Christian community as are Paul's letters.

See: Benziger New Testament Study Series. p. 205

1. Up-to-date historical critical scholarship incorporated?	**Yes**
2. Background information emphasized?	**Yes**
3. Application to personal and family life emphasized?	**Yes**
4. Application to the life and mission of the church included?	**Yes**
5. Application to broader social issues included?	**Yes**
6. Sexist language avoided?	**Yes**
7. Guidance for prayer at group meetings provided?	**No**
8. Discussion questions provided?	**Yes**
9. Practical directions for group leaders provided?	**No**
10. Biblical background for group leaders provided?	**No**
11. Biblical background for group members presumed?	**No**
12. Participants required to prepare for each session?	**Yes**

ADULTS APPROACH "THE REVELATION".

Brethren House, 1985. 68 pp., 8 ½ x 11. $7.50. 7 or 13 sessions.

This is a truly remarkable program. It bypasses all the problems that absorb the attention of most groups studying the Book of Revelation and focuses instead on its poetic power and the underlying messages about God, the power of evil, and the victory of Jesus.

The author presents and applies some excellent exegetical principles. One of these is that "'The Revelation' is not meant to be read silently and analyzed but to be listened to, experienced, and obeyed." Therefore there is much well prepared reading aloud, with time afterwards for participants to journal about the impact of the images on them, followed by time for optional sharing. Participants are guided as to how to listen to this particular kind of poetry.

Another principle is "All interpretation must begin with what it meant to the writer and to his original audience." An exercise is suggested in which participants role play early Christians with diverse attitudes toward the persecution. This prepares participants for listening to Revelation as it would have sounded to the original hearers. It is typical of the Brethren House sensitivity to contemporary issues that a similar exercise asks participants to identify with specific oppressed groups today and listen to Revelation with their ears.

Another exegetical principle is "The book is a revelation of Jesus Christ in the context of worship." Prayer exercises using the text of Revelation help participants to experience the centrality of worship in it. A list is given of Christian hymns which use Revelation.

Through a carefully planned process of study with some basic input and exercises by which participants discover for themselves what is in the text, guided meditation, prayerful listening, journaling, and sharing, the program creates an experience of the power of the Book of Revelation which is so often lost amidst the analysis of the details.

Only the teacher needs a copy of the book. Handout materials for participants may be reproduced. No preparation is necessary for participants, though suggestions are given for work between sessions. The leader, on the other hand, needs teaching skills and considerable preparation. Biblical background would be helpful especially during the sessions dealing with Old Testament background of Revelation, but it is not essential.

The author believes that Revelation was written by the Apostle John, a position most scholars today would reject. However, this is only mentioned in passing and should not dissuade anyone from using this outstanding program.

1. Up-to-date historical critical scholarship incorporated?   **Yes**

2. Background information emphasized?   **Yes**

3. Application to personal and family life emphasized?   **Yes**

4. Application to the life and mission of the church included?   **Yes**

5. Application to broader social issues included?   **Yes**

6. Sexist language avoided?   **Yes**

7. Guidance for prayer at group meetings provided?   **Yes**

8. Discussion questions provided?   **Yes**

9. Practical directions for group leaders provided?   **Yes**

10. Biblical background for group leaders provided?   **Yes**

11. Biblical background for group members presumed?   **Yes**

12. Participants required to prepare for each session?   **No**

THE BOOK OF REVELATION.

William A. Anderson. Benziger New Testament Study Series. Benziger, 1988. imprimatur. 88 pp., 5 ¼ x 8. $4.68.

This is a commentary in the simplest possible terms on the very complicated Book of Revelation. It is based on current scholarship and emphasizes that Revelation is intended to give hope to persecuted Christians, not to be a message of doom about the end of the world. The commentary is mostly concerned to explain the symbols used. Anyone familiar with the Book of Revelation and scholarship on it will not be surprised to hear that even after Father Anderson's explanations the symbols are still not altogether clear.

Bible study groups may find it difficult to carry on lively sessions based on this book, not because of any fault of Father Anderson but because of the difficulty of both understanding and applying the Book of Revelation.

The cover indicates that this commentary also includes the Universal Letters, but this is an error. They are in a different volume of this series.

See: Benziger New Testament Study Series. p. 205

1. Up-to-date historical critical scholarship incorporated?   **Yes**

2. Background information emphasized?   **Yes**

3. Application to personal and family life emphasized?   **No**

4. Application to the life and mission of the church included?   **No**

5. Application to broader social issues included?   **No**

6. Sexist language avoided?   **Yes**

7. Guidance for prayer at group meetings provided?   **No**

8. Discussion questions provided?   **Yes**

9. Practical directions for group leaders provided?   **No**

10. Biblical background for group leaders provided?   **No**

11. Biblical background for group members presumed?   **No**

12. Participants required to prepare for each session?   **Yes**

REVELATION.

Timothy J. Wengert. Men's Bible Study. Augsburg, 1988. Study Book: 48 pp., 4 ½ x 9 ½. $2.85. Leader Guide: 32 pp., 4 ½ x 9 ½. $3.10. 10 sessions.

The Book of Revelation is not the best starting point for a group without extensive biblical background. Its complexities can either discourage people from Bible study altogether or get them fascinated with unsound interpretations. It is particularly difficult to deal with in the kind of group for which this guide was written: people who are not preparing for the sessions and spend only half an hour together.

However, if such a group does decide to study the Book of Revelation, this is an excellent guide for them. The author gives an overview of the different methods of interpretation, which is enough to discourage anyone from being too dogmatic about any particular interpretation. He then focuses on a method which acknowledges the literary form and historical background but focuses on the underlying messages which are still applicable today. From Revelation he finds light thrown on Christian sacraments, prejudice, drugs, the experience of the church in areas where it suffers persecution today, contemporary worship of money, power and the state, conflict of interests between rich and poor nations and between labor and management, etc.

These 10 brief lessons cannot cover the entire Book of Revelation, nor deal with its overall structure, but they do clarify many details which make the book meaningful for today's Christian. They also show up the error in a number of popular misinterpretations.

See: Men's Bible Study Series, p. 219

1. Up-to-date historical critical scholarship incorporated?   **Yes**

2. Background information emphasized?   **No**

3. Application to personal and family life emphasized?   **Yes**

4. Application to the life and mission of the church included?   **Yes**

5. Application to broader social issues included?   **Yes**

6. Sexist language avoided?   **Yes**

7. Guidance for prayer at group meetings provided?   **Yes**

8. Discussion questions provided?   **Yes**

9. Practical directions for group leaders provided?   **Yes**

10. Biblical background for group leaders provided?   **Yes**

11. Biblical background for group members presumed?   **No**

12. Participants required to prepare for each session?   **Yes**

Reviews of Series of Studies

Series of Studies

Benziger Publishing Company.

This series of 12 volumes covering the entire New Testament is designed primarily for private use. However, a creative group leader could adapt it to group use by utilizing the reflection questions for discussion and perhaps adding other questions.

The series is directed to "people who live hectic, busy lives and who do not wish to come home to an evening of heavy reading." It aims to present the basics in non-technical terms, and so to provide a foundation on which future study could be based. The commentary is solidly based on contemporary scholarship. However, even interpretations which frequently shock the uninitiated are presented in a style so low key that few will be shocked. The reassuring atmosphere is enhanced by a picture of Father Anderson in a Roman collar on the back cover of each book.

Each volume contains the text of the Revised New Testament of the New American Bible, broken up into brief segments, each followed by commentary. The commentary consists of a paraphrase of the verses just given, with some helpful information, such as one finds in footnotes, interspersed. There is more information provided in the Gospels and Acts than in the letters. The commentaries show a remarkable grasp of contemporary biblical scholarship translated into very simple terms.

The almost verse by verse treatment does not allow explanations of some more general issues which would be useful for beginners. Neither does it allow for highlighting effectively the more important themes and passages. It is well done to serve the purpose for which it is intended, however.

Important Old Testament background is pointed out, and readers would be well advised to look up the references given.

There are no frills: no attention grabbing format, no illustrations, charts or maps, no suggestions for further reading, no directions for group leaders. Little geographical, historical, or archeological background is included in the commentary. A group might want to have a biblical atlas and other reference books on hand to add these dimensions.

The only attempt to make the commentary more appealing is a story, usually modern, used to introduce each biblical book, and another used in the conclusion to each book.

It will be a challenge for a leader to break the material up into an amount suitable for each session, and to decide which questions to use or whether substitute other questions more likely to interest the group. The review questio provided simply ask for a restatement of the material in the commentary. T reflection questions raise issues about the application of the scripture studied personal and church life.

Because the units are very brief, they could be used even by groups meeting f twenty minutes. Some groups might want to read the scripture and commenta during the session instead of preparing ahead. Many adaptations are possible.

LESS BIBLE STUDIES:
RINGING LIFE EXPERIENCE TO SCRIPTURE STUDY.
gsburg

is remarkable series is designed for use in health care centers and nursing homes. e attractive format features large print and photographs bringing out the special auty of older people.

ch 12 session program has a leader guide and a participant book. The participant ok consists of 12 pages, printed on both sides, which can be torn out for use as ndouts at each session. It is valuable because it enables each one to participate in e responsive prayer and gives each a reminder of the theme for reflection during e week for later use. However, in some situations it will be necessary, and possible, manage without the participant books.

e leader guide is invaluable. It contains 13 pages of superb practical instructions r anyone working with nursing home residents, with emphasis on how to start a ble study group in such a setting. Specific techniques for dealing with the physical d mental problems which challenge the leader of such a group are included. (These pages are repeated in each of the leader guides.) Following are detailed, carefully ought out plans for 12 sessions.

fter individually greeting each participant, the leader starts each session with a sponsive prayer and a hymn. The leader then reads or summarizes a paragraph om the guide introducing the scripture reading. Next, a familiar biblical story is ad aloud. The leader starts discussion with a very carefully constructed series of uestions. The first are totally non-threatening and deal with the story just read. radually the questions move to general applications of the story and finally to ersonal sharing. The life experience questions are planned to strengthen residents' nse of self worth and give meaning to their lives.

he leader guide suggests possible answers to the questions. Just reading through ese would provide anyone with marvelous insights into the real concerns of ersons in nursing homes and new sensitivity to them.

nother paragraph titled "Summary" brings the discussion to an end, again tying e scripture story read to the theme. A hymn, scripture verse, prayer, and blessing nclude the session.

strong and successful effort is made to eliminate denominational bias. The only ay in which Catholics will be at a disadvantage is that they may not be familiar with e hymns. It is nevertheless strongly encouraged that hymns be included because

of their therapeutic value in evoking feelings and because they are a way
encouraging participation. (The leader guide says that some persons unable to spe
can join in singing!) A tape of the suggested hymns can be purchased for $8.98, a
the music is in the leader guide, while words for singing are in the participant's boc
Other hymns could be substituted, of course, but copies and accompaniment wou
have to be arranged.

Though there is a logical flow to each program, each session could stand on its ow
Residents who do not come regularly could still benefit.

In addition to the two programs reviewed in this book, the Bless Bible Seri
includes *Blessed by the Spirit* and *Seasonal Studies*.

The stated purposes are to provide nursing home residents with an experience
meet their particular spiritual needs and deal with their particular questions, and
help them see God at work in their lives. The goals are very well met in th
extraordinary series.

See: * **Blessed by the God of Abraham, Isaac, and Jacob, p. 65**
      Blessed by Jesus, p. 119

Series of Studies

COVENANT BIBLE STUDIES.
Brethren Press

This series claims to be "designed to be applied to life situations. It is not intended to be analytical or technical commentary on the texts. Guidance is provided to assist the group to live into the scriptural story, making bridges between this story and present or future implications...The Body of Christ becomes a reality within the life of the group as each person contributes to the group's study, prayer, and work together. Each one's contribution is needed as the group seeks the meaning of the text...We are vulnerable as we share out of life's experience; in relational Bible study we learn to trust others and to be trustworthy." It is well adapted to its goals of community building and scripture application.

These attractive booklets all have the same format. They provide 10 sessions each. Each session contains a scripture assignment and suggestions for individual preparation, three and a half pages of commentary, discussion questions, and suggestions for action. The discussion questions are very good at connecting the scripture with real issues of today, both personal and broader. The commentary is by a different author in each case, and varies considerably in emphasis.

The introductory booklet, *Forming Bible Study Groups* , deals in a very practical way with the details of starting and leading Bible study groups. It will be useful for group leaders, whether they are using the Covenant Bible Studies or others.

This program was designed for use by small groups within the Church of the Brethren, but is also suitable for Catholic or other groups. It is suggested that groups meet for two hours, including an hour of Bible study and an hour of other kinds of sharing. However, the Bible study alone might be used by groups which can meet only for an hour or even somewhat less.

See: Forming Bible Study Groups, p. 233
   Love and Justice: A Biblical Understanding, p. 51
   The Life of David, p. 87
   * Psalms, p. 99
   Sermon on the Mount, p. 149

DE SALES PROGRAM.
Franciscan Communications

This video adult education program was produced by the Diocese of Baker, Oregon, to meet the needs of a population so scattered that it was difficult to find lecturers to come to all the parishes. Some, though not all, of the segments deal with the Bible.

The strength of this program is in the professionally prepared videos. Clever visual aids assist the teaching process immensely. Also, during the lectures many pictures (classical works of art, scenery, scenes from daily life, etc.) are shown. The connection of the picture with the words being spoken is not always completely clear, but the general effect is far less boring than watching a lecturer through an entire lecture.

The weakness of the program is that it is not geared to encourage group participation in the learning process to a very high degree. After the information has been provided by the 50 minute video lecture, 20 minutes are allowed for group discussion, and two questions are provided. This is not a program in which participants actually study the biblical text together.

A group wishing to extend the discussion time could do so, but would have to devise additional discussion questions or group exercises. A few exercises in which participants actually use their Bibles are recommended to be done at home, but this seems to be tacked on rather than an essential part of the program. A creative leader could utilize the exercises and articles provided to extend the sharing time. In this case, the length of the session could be extended to two hours, or the lecture could be divided at the "Break" point and used for two sessions.

Each 90 minute session consists in a 10 minute reflective exercise, using a journal and group sharing, 25 minutes of video input, a break, another 25 minutes of video input, 20 minutes of discussion, and a 10 minute video conclusion. A program hostess appears with the guest speaker at the beginning of the video and for the final 10 minutes. She represents the ordinary Catholic and raises questions and concerns which many participants will have. At the end of each session she also encourages participants to some practical exercise of faith based on the session. She adds elements of continuity and dialogue throughout.

One Facilitator Guide applies to all De Sales programs. Every facilitator should read this carefully. It gives a clear job description and list of "do's" and "don'ts" for facilitators. There is plenty of detailed practical advise about organizing, recruiting, and leading. It also includes models of useful forms and certificates of completion which can be reproduced.

Each participant needs a Participant Manual. For each session this contains som[e] suggested background articles, journal space for the opening reflection, an outli[ne] of the lectures with space for taking notes during the videos, and suggestions for [a]n activity during the coming week . Helpful charts and maps are also provided [as] needed.

The speakers are varied and generally good. Their use of visual aids is particular[ly] fine. The lectures aim to simplify contemporary biblical scholarship and relate it [to] Catholic tradition and post-Vatican II Catholic experience. They impart informatic[on] in a way that will support the faith of participants. Technical jargon is avoided. F[or] the sake of simplicity, the diversity of scholarly views on some issues is n[ot] recognized.

The articles included are from a wide variety of contemporary Catholic autho[rs] writing for a popular audience. They are brief and easy to read. The lecture an[d] discussion will make sense whether a participant chooses to read the articles or n[ot].

Due to the variety of authors and speakers, the program is inconsistent regarding t[he] use of sexist language.

Each Participant Guide includes an annotated bibliography (which is well don[e] indicating levels of difficulty, plus a separate list of works more focused on praye[r]. Many of the books from which selections were included in the suggested reading i[n] the manual are listed in the bibliography as possibilities for further reading. The[se] bibliographies are valuable resources even apart from the program.

This reviewer considered *The Writings of St.Paul* the best of the series.

See: **Basic Tools for Bible Study, p. 15**
  The Story of the Old Testament Covenant, p. 75
  The Living Gospels, p. 133
  * The Writings of St.Paul, p. 189

Series of Studies

FRIENDSHIP BIBLE STUDY SERIES.
Augsburg Fortress

These programs are designed for neighborhood, ecumenical, or congregational small groups who wish to spend one hour together in biblical reflection without becoming involved in technical analysis or academic research. The goal is to enter into the scriptural text, finding its connections to personal, congregational, and public life. There is also a strong emphasis on forming friendships among participants. Suggestions are made for study and action between sessions, but even those who do not prepare would be able to participate.

This is a Lutheran publication, and hymns, Bible translations, and resources listed are different from those familiar to Catholics. However, there is no serious reason why it could not be used by Christians of any denomination.

Participants are asked to read a biblical passage carefully, write brief answers to questions in the workbook, share their insights and experience with each other, and listen carefully to each other, valuing diversity rather than trying to reach agreement.

A small amount of very simple background material is provided, without any mention of areas where scholars disagree among themselves. Helpful cross references to other parts of scripture are also given.

Sensitivity is shown to justice and feminist issues. Masculine pronouns are not used for God except in quotations.

The Leader's Guide contains slightly more background material and some suggestions for group facilitation. The leader would not need any special biblical background.

These are good programs for post-Renew, ecumenical, and other groups where a small amount of scripture is used as a starting point for faith sharing and community building.

See: Jonah and Ruth, p. 71
      * Isaiah, p. 93
      Proverbs, p. 97
      Parables, p. 139
      1,2,3 John, p. 191

LIFE APPLICATION BIBLE STUDIES.
Tyndale House Publishers

Each volume includes:

- The complete text of the biblical book. Some volumes use the Living Bible version without giving the unwary reader any indication that it is a paraphrase which interprets rather than translates. Other volumes use the New International Version.

- Abundant footnotes. These sometimes provide background information (always from a fundamentalist point of view) but often are sermonettes. Charts of useful information in easy to remember form are also included. Much of the information is quite contrary to the findings of historical critical study.

- Thirteen very well designed lessons. These are in an attractive workbook form. The first questions evoke the reader's own experience which will assist in interpreting the text. Other questions help in analyzing and applying the text. Each lesson ends with questions titled MORE. These broaden the study, often connecting the passage being studied to other parts of scripture. Many groups may find these MORE questions the best for discussion. The questions are well planned to assist the student to find meaning in the scripture passage; they do not try to force a specific answer. Unfortunately, some information is interspersed among the questions, and it is no more reliable than the information in the footnotes.

The editors claim that 75% of this material is oriented to application. In general, this is excellent material, suitable for Christians of any tradition. Application is made to personal, family, and business life, and also to broader social issues. Students are challenged to critique the affluent society and show concern for the poor.

There seems to be an effort to avoid sexist language, but it is not carried out consistently. In general the sensitivity to women's issues is more than one expects in evangelical publications.

Unfortunately, it is difficult for Catholic or mainline groups to use these books because the excellent lesson plans are mingled with so much misinformation, and in many cases the Living Bible paraphrase is used. However, a biblically educated group leader who is creating discussion questions for a specific group would benefit greatly from using the questions as models.

Series of Studies

LITTLE ROCK SCRIPTURE STUDY PROGRAM.
The Liturgical Press

Since 1974 the Diocese of Little Rock has been developing this program of scriptural prayer and study for parishes. It is now published through Liturgical Press and is probably the most widely used Catholic program in the United States.

Four elements are essential for each session: daily personal study in preparation, sharing in a small group, a lecture (live, audio taped, or video taped), and prayer. Its clear structure is an asset for many groups.

The personal study consists of a reflective reading of a section of scripture and the commentary on it in the *Collegeville Bible Commentary* (p. 231) and answering questions in the Study Guide. (A separate Answer Guide is available in case help is needed for the factual questions.) The questions are non-threatening. Some aid in remembering what is said in the text or commentary, some in interpreting it, and some in applying it to modern life. Some questions require the use of cross references.

Participants are encouraged to have the *Dictionary of the Bible* by McKenzie (p. 231) available for study. The workbook format of the Study Guide provides space for writing answers, but many will find it too cramped and prefer to use a notebook. Each participant is expected to spend 30 minutes daily in this preparation, though people who spend less still seem to gain some benefit from the program.

Fifty five minutes of each session is spent in discussing the assigned questions in small groups. Leaders encourage participants to share their personal thoughts in an atmosphere of openness and love.

After the group sharing, 25 minutes are spent listening to a lecture on what has been discussed. Ideally, a competent local person gives this lecture. However, if such a person cannot be found, audio and video lectures are available. The video lectures show the speaker, but also insert shots of contemporary life, art work, maps, and charts listing the main points of the lecture.

Conversational prayer is also an important part of each session.

Though a little scholarly background is available in the commentary provided, this is definitely a study *of* the Bible, not a study *about* the Bible. Academics are kept in the background, and participants are urged to find the meaning of the scripture for themselves.

In contrast to many programs, Little Rock participants cover the Bible book by book reading each book completely. Many groups have continued for years.

Foundational programs are:
Introduction to the Bible
The Acts of the Apostles
Synoptic Gospels
Paul's Captivity Letters
Exodus

Further programs available are:
First Samuel, Second Samuel
Jeremiah
Isaiah
Genesis
The Book of Revelation
Matthew
Mark
Luke
John and the Johannine Epistles
First Corinthians
Second Corinthians
Hebrews and James
Galatians and Romans
Psalms I
Psalms II
The Birth of Christ
The Passion and Resurrection Narratives

The program is planned to be led by lay people with no previous experience c scripture, but five sessions of leadership training are required to prepare them Material for this training is available in audio or video form. See *Little Rock Scriptur Study: Coordinator's Manual.* This manual also includes information about organiza tion, recruitment, children's programs, etc. When the parish program begins, th leaders meet for one hour before each group session to prepare and to support eac other.

This is a good program for Catholic groups who have committed and trained leader and members willing to prepare for weekly sessions and to share their faitl but not wishing too much of an intellectual challenge.

See: The Acts of the Apostles, p. 167
Little Rock Scripture Study: Coordinator's Manual, p. 233

Series of Studies

MEN'S BIBLE STUDY SERIES.
Augsburg

These are 30 minute Bible studies which do not require preparation by participants. The Bible passages studied are brief and can be read during the session. The intent is to aid men in understanding scripture, in discovering and responding to opportunities for ministry, and in sharing with and supporting other men in the group.

The studies are suitable for men of any Christian denomination, though their Lutheran origin is seen in the use of quotations from Martin Luther and prayers from the Lutheran Book of Worship. Books which are recommended for extra enrichment are generally Protestant, but a leader could easily substitute others. There are many references to Baptism and Communion and to congregational worship.

Interestingly, sexist language is avoided and God is not referred to as masculine, except in quotations. There is generally a sensitivity to feminist concerns. Apart from the title, there seems to be little reason that the series could not be used by women.

Each booklet includes a brief introduction and 10 sessions. Each session contains one or two brief prayers to be said by the group, references to the basic scripture verses being studied and several cross references to related scripture passages, a small amount of commentary, and several questions for discussion. The scripture passages and commentary are to be read aloud during the group session. Participants would need Bibles to find the references.

The goal is practical application rather than academic study. Even the background provided in the leader's guide is elementary. Neither leader nor participants are presumed to have much scripture background.

These are very practical booklets for groups which want to give half an hour to scripture study during breakfast, lunch, or other meetings.

See: **Amos and Hosea, p. 89**
Psalms, p. 101
1 and 2 Corinthians, p. 175
Hebrews, p. 179
Revelation, p. 201

Series of Studies

PAULIST BIBLE STUDY PROGRAM.
Paulist Press

This program utilizes contemporary methods of adult education to enable adults to learn the insights of scholarship about the Bible and also to learn to use the Bible in their own prayer and reflection. Both ecclesial tradition and historical critical study are utilized. Catholic church documents are quoted frequently.

Each segment of this program provides eight sessions. Each session consists of:
1. Opening prayer (5 minutes)
2. A review of the material participants studied in preparation for the session (25 minutes)
3. A video presentation (20 minutes)
4. A learning activity (25 minutes)
5. Faith sharing (25 minutes)
6. Closing prayer (10 minutes).

After each session an abundance of suggestions are made for personal journaling and additional reading. In addition, substantial reading from the required textbook and the Bible is assigned in preparation for the next session.

Besides Bibles, four materials are necessary: Leader's Manuals, Workbooks (one for each participant), textbooks (a couple might share one), and a video. All are visually attractive and show care and expertise in their preparation.

The Leader's Manual provides detailed instructions for the group leader. It also contains five excellent pages on contemporary theories of adult education. (These pages are identical in the manuals for the two segments reviewed in this book.) For each session the manual repeats all the material in the participant's Workbook, plus a great deal of biblical information which might be needed in discussing the review questions or doing the learning activity, and practical suggestions for making every part of the session proceed smoothly. Additional readings for the leader are also suggested, usually from the *New Jerome Biblical Commentary* (p. 231).

The Workbook, which each participant needs, contains a list of readings to be done in preparation, the text of the prayer services (except songs), review questions to assist in understanding the assigned readings, the instructions needed for the learning activity and the faith sharing, a simple format for taking notes while watching the video, and follow-up suggestions for further reading and journaling.

Each participant also needs the college level textbook from which the assigned readings are selected. To do the additional suggested readings, a considerable collection of books would be needed.

A single video contains the eight 15 minute segments needed for the eight sessions. Each video shows Father Lawrence Boadt, C.S.P. and Maria Harris presenting information. It is enlivened by frequent glimpses of art work of many styles or biblical themes, scenes of the Holy Land, scenes from everyday life, and actors who recite sections of scripture or occasionally present a kind of mini-drama. Charts and maps are also well used. Probably few people will actually understand the connection of all these visuals with the topic being treated, but the abundance of visual stimuli will benefit some types of learners.

In fact, this many faceted program offers something for everyone. However, to succeed it requires participants who are willing to enter into the entire package: regular attendance, hours of heavy reading in preparation, sharing both right brain and left brain activities with the group, and revealing their personal life in the group faith sharing.

The publisher feels that no special biblical education is necessary for the leader, but this reviewer suspects that a leader without substantial biblical background would have to spend a prohibitive amount of time in preparation each week, unless the group included a biblical resource person who could help with questions about the biblical content. The leader also needs considerable facilitation skills. A song leader and song books are also needed.

Respect for women's concerns shows throughout. Generic masculines are not used except in quotations. Masculine pronouns for God are avoided in prayer services but not consistently elsewhere.

Of the two programs reviewed in this book, *Jesus and the Gospels* seems considerably less difficult than *Israel Becomes a People* and might be the better one for beginners.

Extensive knowledge of contemporary biblical scholarship and contemporary adult education methodology is evident in every part of the material provided. Groups willing to make the necessary commitment and blessed with well qualified leaders will find these programs outstanding.

See: Israel Becomes a People, p. 79
      * Jesus and the Gospels, p. 127

Series of Studies

QUESTIONS OF CHRISTIANS.
ACTA Publications

This program aims to explore the questions being asked by Christians today and those which were asked by the Christians for whom the evangelists first wrote. It searches for answers in the gospels which are still relevant, based on the conviction that "The basic experiences of the human heart that struggles and reaches out for God are always the same no matter what person in which particular time and place has them. It is to these experiences that this program addresses itself."

Though this program uses audio tapes, it is not to be confused with programs which use taped lectures in place of live lecturers. This is a very carefully structured program which uses short taped segments in highly creative ways, but emphasizes group sharing.

Preparation is not required. A typical session begins with a ten minute review of the previous session, followed by a 10 minute audio tape. (See individual reviews for the contents of these tapes, which differ greatly in the four programs.)

Then participants are invited to reflect on their personal experiences (which will later provide entry into the scriptural texts). The booklet provides questions such as, "Suppose you were trying to help a friend get to know you better and to understand you better, what stories from your childhood about your parents, your neighborhood, your ancestry, your education, your economic circumstances would you tell that person? What could those stories reveal about you?" "When you read in a newspaper accounts of atrocities committed in countries involved in civil turmoil, or of injustice to innocent people in this or other countries, what is your usual reaction?" After five minutes of silent reflection and journaling on these questions, 15 to 25 minutes are spent sharing in groups of four or five, then five to 10 minutes in sharing with the total group.

Then the second brief taped segment is played to provide background for the biblical theme for the week. Selected gospel passages relating to that theme are read aloud by group members while others jot down reflections on the readings. Then "Questions for Reflection and Growth" are discussed in the same format as the questions on personal experience (silent reflection, small group, large group). These questions call for application of the scripture message to life. They are open ended, leaving participants free to search in their own way.

The small sharing groups are to change constantly, so that all members become acquainted with each other.

Participants are urged to continue the search begun during the session by reading further in the gospel and reading seven to ten pages of commentary provided in their books after each session. This is informational material based on contemporary scholarship, but avoiding technical terminology. Only those who actually use this commentary will gain any substantial knowledge of biblical scholarship on the gospels. Others will still benefit from reading and discussing in the group.

The strong point of this program is the excellent questions which tie scripture to life in very realistic ways. Some groups will find the 20 minute sharing periods too brief, but the purpose is not to exhaust the material but to provide a starter for a lifelong process of reflection. The audio segments are well planned to spark personal reflection and discussion rather than replacing them.

This program can be used by groups with no biblical background, or by groups which do have such background but wish to focus on general themes and application to life rather than doing a verse by verse study. It requires a leader and group comfortable with a highly structured approach.

Scripture training is not essential for the leader but would be very helpful, especially during the review of the previous session. Participants should be free to raise questions from their reading of the commentary at this time, and it would be best if the leader or some other member of the group could assist as needed. Very convenient cards with an outline of each session are provided to assist the leader in keeping the group on schedule.

Of the four programs, this reviewer found that the one on Matthew is the best and that the one on Mark is the least useful.

See: Questions of Christians: Vol. 1, Mark's Response, p. 153
    * Questions of Christians: Vol. 2, Matthew's Response, p. 147
    Questions of Christians: Vol. 3, Luke's Response, p. 159
    Questions of Christians: Vol. 4, John's Response, p. 163

Series of Studies

SCRIPTURE SHARE AND PRAYER.
Scripture Share and Prayer

Mary Mauren has been a very popular teacher and organizer of scripture programs in the Archdiocese of Seattle since 1974. Her greatest strength is in her lively storytelling and her ability to share her own life experience and faith in a way that puts listeners in touch with their own experiences. The materials which she developed were at one time published by Sheed and Ward, but can now be obtained directly from the author.

She begins, "The vision of Scripture Share and Prayer is that of the People of God on a safe and caring pilgrimage where study is aimed at developing a working knowledge of scripture in order to form a biblical spirituality. The materials incarnate the vision. Therefore, the student lessons are simply study guides that help to focus on the journey process, not to focus on arriving at the 'definition' of the 'right' answer."

Mary Mauren's vision is of a parish program involving a highly developed community of trained facilitators. Full information about leadership training for such a program, children's programs connected with it, etc., can be obtained from Scripture Share and Prayer.

However, the materials can be adapted to use by a small group with only one or two leaders. Three segments have been reviewed in this book for such use. The segments here reviewed are those which are recommended to be done first; other segments available are:

Exile/Post-Exile Prophets
Paul's Captivity & Pastoral Letters
Introduction to the Pentateuch
Synoptic Gospels
Wisdom Literature
Writings of John.

Some segments are available on video tape.

The program is well named. Strong emphasis is placed on community building and on prayer. However, the study element is also strong, with heavy emphasis on historical background.

Except for *Scripture Foundations*, the method used is the "Discovery Method." Each week participants are given at least a dozen study questions to be answered from the text. These are not simplistic questions, and will require hours of intensive study. They are generally open-ended questions which can be answered in more than one way and will stimulate good discussion. Some application questions and prayer suggestions are included. Only after this in depth personal study do participants discuss the material in small groups. If a lecture (live, or by audio or video tape) is included, it comes after its topic has been discussed in the small groups.

The audio tapes are of Mary Mauren's lectures. These hour long lectures combine a great deal of content based on contemporary biblical scholarship with homey illustrations from the author's life as wife and mother of eight and her own faith witness. She avoids sexist language, and does not use masculine pronouns for God. Mauren is an excellent popularizer of scholarship. She gains her audience's attention by vivid storytelling both of the biblical stories themselves and of contemporary events which she ties in with the scripture. The tapes have the usual weakness of anything taped in a live situation: occasionally there are breaks during which students are asking questions which are not audible or the teacher is writing on the board. However, they are generally easy to listen to. A group could listen to the entire lecture or have one member listen to it and serve as a resource during the discussion.

The study guides come in a looseleaf binder, and can be reproduced for group use. Each study guide contains about a page of background material and two pages of questions. Handouts are also included, such as timelines, maps, charts, and forms to use in reflective exercises.

The reviewer highly recommends that *Ministry Formation* be done first, then *Scripture Foundations*, then *Pre-Exilic Prophets*, then *Acts--Paul's Early and Great Letters*.

This is a complex program, suitable for people willing to put much time and energy into community building and study and blessed with competent and dynamic leadership. They will find it a rich experience.

See: Scripture Foundations. p. 31
Pre-exilic Prophets, p. 95
Acts--Paul's Early and Great Letters, p. 169
Ministry Formation, p. 233
Creating Communities of Good News, p. 233

Series of Studies

SMALL-GROUP BIBLE STUDY.
Augsburg Fortress

These inexpensive booklets provide questions for discussion in an attractive format. Discussion groups of eight are recommended, but the questions could be used even by groups of two or three. Some questions aim at leading to a careful reading of the text; others at applying the text to life. None assume that participants have any knowledge of scripture or of biblical scholarship. Scarcely any background information is provided, but the questions could be very helpful for a group that simply wants to take the scripture at face value and search out how it can be applied in their own lives.

The participant is often referred to related passages in other parts of scripture and occasionally to a Bible dictionary.

Two hour sessions are recommended, and these consist entirely in discussion of the questions, except for a brief opening and closing prayer. Since there are a great many questions, the leader would have to exercise discernment in deciding which ones to use. Since the discussion questions are linked with specific brief passages, it is possible that a group without any previous preparation could discuss them, simply reading the relevant verses aloud before the discussion. However, the recommended procedure is for participants to read the scripture and reflect on the questions in advance.

Occasional references to Luther's writings and use of prayers from the Lutheran Book of Worship indicate that these questions were prepared for Lutherans, but there is no serious reason why they could not be used by Catholics and members of other denominations.

In view of the lack of background information, the program would probably best suit groups where at least one member had enough background to answer questions that arose. A good Bible dictionary and other reference books should also be available.

See: * Peacemaking, p. 53
     Flight to Freedom, p. 77
     Mary, p. 135
     1, 2 Thessalonians, p. 177

Series of Studies

CHARLES R. SWINDOLL BIBLE STUDY GUIDES.
Insight for Living, distributed by Word Publishing Company

This series of 48 books is by an evangelical preacher who also offers a daily radio program. It is intended for use, either individually or in groups, by Evangelical Christians. It has great appeal because of its attractive format, low price, lively style, and abundance of practical advice for prayer and for personal and family life.

The methodology is the same in each book. A scripture reference is given at the beginning of each lesson, but it is unclear whether students are really expected to read it. This is a series which tells one what the scripture means, rather than enabling one to find meaning for oneself in the scripture. The main element of each lesson is a commentary in the style of a very lively sermon, with abundance of contemporary stories, illustrations from history, and psychological insights. Then meditation or journal writing exercises are recommended to assist in analyzing and applying the text. Many exercises involve paraphrasing, using a concordance, highlighting certain words in different colors in one's Bible, etc. One exercise, for instance, has the student list the 15 verbs in a passage, define them, and then try to decide how the definitions might apply in the context. These are very simple, left brain exercises, which anyone with sufficient time could do. For beginners with poor educational background they could give needed encouragement and a sense of accomplishment.

If two or more people did the exercises, they would probably find it fruitful to share their work afterwards. The more probing application questions would make good sharing material for some groups, though there are few questions specifically geared to group discussion.

Occasionally there are sections called "Digging Deeper" with lists of other, mainly Evangelical, writings on a topic.

Catholics will have difficulty with the extremely literal and dogmatic interpretations of scripture and the total ignoring of historical critical scholarship. Old Testament passages are applied to Jesus without regard for their meaning in their original contexts. Fundamentalist beliefs such as the Rapture and the assured salvation of those who have been "born again" are read into biblical texts which Catholic and mainline Protestant scholars would interpret very differently. Terminology is used as in the Evangelical vocabulary and may occasionally be misleading or offensive to those of other traditions.

Though the emphasis is always on practical application of the text, this application is generally limited to the private or ecclesiastical sphere. There is no effort to apply scripture to issues of social justice or global affairs. No respect is shown for religious traditions other than Christian. No attempt is made to avoid sexist language. In fact, feminism is listed as one of the causes of deterioration in family life.

The problems of using this series are not equally present in each book. In view of the methodology which is particularly well designed for beginners of limited educational background looking for immediate practical applications, some volumes which do not deal with controversial theological issues are reviewed in this book.

See: Joseph, from Pit to Pinnacle, p. 83
    Hand Me Another Brick: A Study of Nehemiah, p. 85

Reference Books Recommended for Bible Study Groups

Annotated Bibles:

The Catholic Study Bible. New American Bible, with Revised New Testament. Oxford University Press, 1990. 2228 pp., 7 x 10. $29.95 Hardcover.

The New Catholic Study Bible, St. Jerome Edition. Today's English Version with Deuterocanonicals. Catholic Bible Press, Thomas Nelson, Inc., 1985. 1680 pp., 6 x 9. $29.95. Hardcover. This is neither as new nor as useful as the one published by Oxford.

The New Jerusalem Bible. Doubleday, 1985. 2108 pp., 6½ x 9½. $24.95. Hardcover.

The New Oxford Annotated Bible with the Apocrypha. New Revised Standard Version. Oxford University Press, 1991. 2112 pp., 7 x 9. $37.95. Hardcover.

Bible Dictionaries:

Dictionary of the Bible. John L. McKenzie. Macmillan, 1965. 954 pp., 6 x 9. $14.95. Paper.

Harper's Bible Dictionary. Harper San Francisco, 1985. 1178 pp., 6½ x 9½. $31.95 Hardcover.

Bible Commentaries:

The Collegeville Bible Commentary. Liturgical Press, 1989. 1301 pp., 7 x 10. $45.00 Hardcover. This is the same commentary which is available in separate booklets, but in the single volume version the biblical text is not included.

Harper's Bible Commentary. Harper San Francisco, 1988. 1326 pp., 6½ x 9½. $33.95. Hardcover.

The New Jerome Biblical Commentary. Prentice Hall, 1990. 1484 pp., 7 x 10. $69.95 Hardcover, (more technical than the above two commentaries).

Bible Atlases:

The Collegeville Bible Study Atlas. Liturgical Press, 1990. 20 pp., 9 ½ x 13. $5.95. Paper.

Hammond's Atlas of the Bible Lands. Harry Thomas Frank. Hammond, 1984. 48 pp., 9 x 12. $6.00. Paper.

Miscellaneous:

The Cotton Patch Versions by Clarence Jordan.
These are paraphrases which retell the New Testament story as if it had happened in the southern United States today. Very useful for injecting a note of humor and a new perspective on selected passages.

> **The Cotton Patch Version of Hebrews and the General Epistles.** New Win Publishing, 1973. 93 pp., 5 ½ x 8 ½. $4.95. Paper.

> **The Cotton Patch Version of Luke and Acts.** New Win Publishing, 1969. 159 pp., 5 ½ x 8 ½. $4.95. Paper.

> **The Cotton Patch Version of Matthew and John.** New Win Publishing, 1970. 128 pp., 5 ½ x 8 ½. $4.95. Paper. Only the first eight chapters of John are included.

> **The Cotton Patch Version of Paul's Epistles.** New Win Publishing, 1968. 158 pp., 5 ½ x 8 ½. $4.95. Paper.

Books by Mark Link, S.J.: These books are generally used as textbooks for high school students, but can be a valuable resource for any group because of the abundance and variety of quotations connected with each part of the Bible.

> **These Stones Will Shout: A New Voice for the Old Testament.** Tabor, 1983. 236 pp, 8 x 9. $10.95. Paper.

> **The Seventh Trumpet: The Good News Proclaimed.** Tabor, 1978. 208 pp., 8 x 9. $10.95. Paper.

> **Lord, Who Are You? The Story of Paul and the Early Church.** Tabor, 1982. 214 pp., 9 x 8. $10.95. Paper.

Harper's Bible Pronunciation Guide. Harper San Francisco, 1989. 170 pp., 6 x 9. $15.95. Hardcover.

Psalms Anew: In Inclusive Language. Nancy Schreck, O.S.F. and Maureen Leach, O.S.F. St. Mary's Press, 1986. 200 pp., 6 x 9. $6.95. Paper. Useful for groups which want to use the psalms for prayer and prefer a version from which sexist language has been removed.

Serendipity Bible for Groups. New International Version. Lyman Coleman, Dietrich Gruen. Serendipity House, 1989. 1644 pp., 6 ½ x 9. $9.95. Paper. Includes discussion questions for every part of the Bible. These should be selected by a person with biblical background, as theological bias is occasionally built into the questions. This is a Protestant translation, which does not include the deuterocanonical books. Information provided in introductions often does not take mainline modern scholarship into account.

Workbook for Lectors and Gospel Readers. Year B. Graziano Marcheschi with Nancy Seitz Marcheschi. Liturgy Training Publications, 1990. 176 pp., 8 ½ x 11. $8.00. Paper. Commentary on the Sunday readings with practical advice for anyone proclaiming the readings.

Leadership Training:

Called to Lead: A Handbook for Facilitators of Bible Study Groups. Guy Lajoie and Doug McCarthy. Diocese of London, Ontario, Guided Study Programs in the Catholic Faith, 1988. 55 pp., 5 ½ x 8 ½. $4.95. (Canadian).

Creating Communities of Good News: A Facilitator's Handbook. Mary Mauren. Scripture Share and Prayer. 58 pp., 8 ½ x 11. $12.50.

Forming Bible Study Groups. Steve Clapp and Gerald W. Peterson. Brethren Press, 1990. 31 pp., 5 ½ x 8 ½. $3.95.

Little Rock Scripture Study: Coordinator's Manual. Liturgical Press, 1987. 64 pp., 8 ½ x 11. $5.00. Audio Lectures (5 cassettes) $30.00. Video Lectures (1 cassette) $60.00.

Ministry Formation. Mary Mauren. Scripture Share and Prayer, 1985. 69 pp., 8 ½ x 11, in looseleaf folder and 5 audiotapes. $50.

Acknowledgments

In 1980, Archbishop James V. Casey heard the cry of his people hungering for a better understanding of the word of God. His response was to found the Catholic Biblical School of the Archdiocese of Denver. It is because of his faith in me in naming me the director charged with turning his vision into a reality that I developed the background to do this book.

The Archdiocese of Denver granted me a leave of absence to do this work, and my competent associate Steve Mueller assumed the directorship of the Catholic Biblical School while I was gone. The entire staff generously accepted additional responsibilities during this period. They also provided immensely valuable moral support and advice on matters from theology to computer repairs. My eternal thanks to Steve Mueller, Ph.D.; Angeline Hubert, O.S.B.; Dorothy Jonaitis, O.P.; Kathy McGovern; Nancy Hoff, R.S.M.; and Helen Williams.

Fr. Gerard Weber, a well-known pioneer in adult religious education, was instrumental in securing the grant from the Foundation for Adult Catechetical Teaching Aids which allowed me the time to complete this project. I thank both him and the Foundation for their support. Fr. Weber was the one who recognized the need for this project and provided invaluable guidance from the beginning.

Gregory Augustine Pierce, co-publisher and editor of ACTA Publications gave me several key suggestions that allowed me to put this book into manageable and useful form, and Mary Buckley, Sr. Rita Benz, B.V.M., and Jean Lachowicz of the ACTA Publications staff did a great job on editing and design.

Fr. Eugene LaVerdiere, S.S.S., one of the giants of modern biblical scholarship, graciously served as a consultant to this project and contributed the Foreward, for which I am humbly grateful.

Thanks also to the students and graduates of the Catholic Biblical School, whose questions showed me the need for this work and whose love and enthusiasm supported me through it, as well as to members of the Bible study groups throughout the country who shared with me evaluations of programs they had personally experienced.

I also appreciate the many publishers who gave advice, encouragement, and review copies of their programs.

Finally, Mary Ann Pitchford volunteered her assistance with typing and proofreading, and Chuck Boyer generously shared his computer expertise. My thanks to them and to everyone who has made this book possible.

List of Publishers

ACTA Publications
4848 N. Clark St.
Chicago, IL 60640-4711

Augsburg Fortress
426 S. Fifth St.
Box 1209
Minneapolis, MN 55440

Ave Maria Press
Notre Dame, IN 46556-0428

Benziger Publishing Co.
15319 Chatsworth St.
Mission Hills, CA 91346-9609

Brethren House
6301 56th Ave., N.
St. Petersburg, FL 33709

Brethren Press
1451 Dundee Ave.
Elgin, IL 60120

Wm. C. Brown
Religious Education Dept.
2460 Kerper Blvd.
Dubuque, IA 52001

The Catholic Home Study Institute
9 Loudoun St., SE
Leesburg, VA 22075

Crossroad Publishing Co.
370 Lexington Ave.
New York, NY 10017

Diocese of London
Guided Study Programs
P.O. Box 2400
London, Ontario
CANADA N6A 4G3

Doubleday and Company
666 Fifth Ave.
New York, NY 10103

Franciscan Communications
1229 S. Santee St.
Los Angeles, CA 90015

Friendship Press
475 Riverside Drive
New York, NY 10115

Gospel Light Curriculum
2300 Knoll Drive
Ventura, CA 93003

Hammond, Inc.
515 Valley St.
Maplewood, NJ 07040

Harper San Francisco
Icehouse One-401
151 Union St.
San Francisco, CA 94111-1299

Hi-Time Publishing Corp.
P.O. Box 13337
Milwaukee, WI 53213-0337

Intervarsity Press
Box F
Downers Grove, IL 60515

Liguori Publications
One Liguori Drive
Liguori, MO 63057-9999

The Liturgical Press
St. John's Abbey
Collegeville, MN 56321-7077

Liturgy Training Publications
1800 N. Hermitage Ave.
Chicago, IL 60622-1101

Macmillan Company
866 Third Ave.
New York, NY 10022

Morehouse Publishing Co.
78 Danbury Road
Wilton, CT 06897

Thomas Nelson
Nelson Place at Elm Hill Pike
P.O. Box 141000
Nashville, TN 37214-1000

New Win Publishing, Inc.
Box 384C. R.R.1, Rte 173W
Hampton, NJ 08827

Oxford University Press
200 Madison Ave.
New York, NY 10016

The Pastoral Press
Veritas Publications
220 Sheridan St. N.W.
Washington, DC 20011

Paulist Press
997 MacArthur Blvd.
Mahwah, NJ 07430

Prentice Hall Press
5 Columbus Circle
New York, NY 10023

St. Anthony Messenger Press
1615 N. Republic St.
Cincinnati, OH 45210

St. Mary's Press
Terrace Heights
Winona, MN 55987-0560

Scripture Share and Prayer
16126 4th St.
Bellevue, WA 98008

Serendipity House Publishing
P.O. Box 462
Port Washington, NY 11050

Harold Shaw Publishers
Box 567
Wheaton, IL 60189

Tabor Publishing
One DLM Park
P.O. Box 7000
Allen, TX 75002

Treehaus Communications, Inc.
P.O. Box 249
Loveland, OH 45140

Tyndale House Publishers
351 Executive Drive
Box 80
Wheaton, IL 60189-0080

Word, Inc.
5221 N. O'Connor Blvd.
Suite 1000
Irving, TX 75039

ndex by Author, Title, and Series

he following listing for each title or series gives the page number of the review of hat publication. Items are cross-referenced within each review. In programs having nore than two authors, their names are not listed. Titles beginning with a numeral e.g., 1 and 2 CORINTHIANS) are listed under the next word in the title (e.g., CORINTHIANS). Titles preceded by asterisk below appear on list of Fifteen avorites found on page 5.

Form for Readers' Response

PICKING THE "RIGHT" BIBLE STUDY PROGRAM is intended to be an annual publication. The author will attempt to keep the book current by continuing to review new material and by updating existing reviews. Please help prepare the next edition by providing your reactions to this one.

1. What features do you find particularly helpful?

2. What additional information would you like to have?

3. List other individual adult Bible study programs or series of studies which you think should be reviewed.

    Title   Author   Publisher

4. Identify any factual mistakes in the book (please give exact page number).

5. Share any disagreements you have with the author's judgments.

6. Make any other comments you wish.

(Optional):

Your Name:_____

Church or Organization: _____

Address: _____

City/State/Zip:_____

Please return to: HOW TO PICK THE "RIGHT" BIBLE STUDY PROGRAM
                    ACTA Publications
                    4848 N. Clark Street
                    Chicago, IL 60640